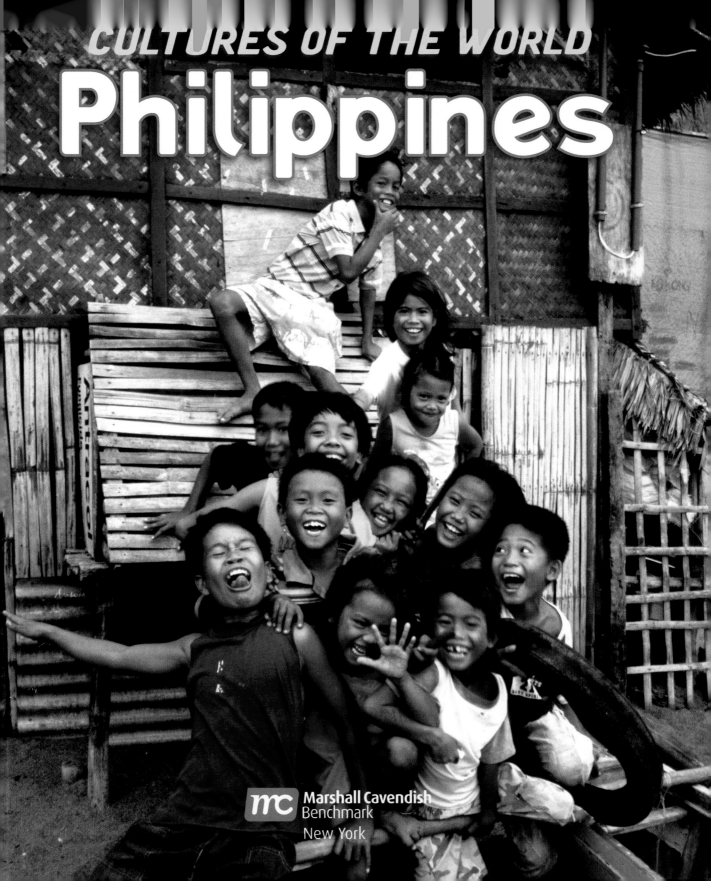

CULTURES OF THE WORLD

Philippines

mc **Marshall Cavendish**
Benchmark
New York

PICTURE CREDITS

Cover: © Tom Cockrem/Photolibrary
Bradley Ambrose/Getty Images: 16 • Carl Mydans/Time & Life Pictures/Getty Images: 66 • Cathy Finch/Lonely Planet Images: 70 • ChinaFotoPress/Getty Images: 32 • David Greedy/Getty Images: 60 • David Greedy/Lonely Planet Images: 85 • Edwin Tuyay/Bloomberg/Getty Images: 36 • Eric Wheater/Lonely Planet Images: 7, 22, 45, 54, 76, 91, 101 • Felix Hug/Lonely Planet Images: 73, 100, 112 • Fleurent/PhotoCuisine/Corbis: 131 • Getty Images/ Photolibrary: 3, 11, 12, 13, 20, 24, 28, 50, 52, 64, 77, 81, 92 • Greg Elms/Lonely Planet Images: 80, 83 • Inmagine: 1, 9, 14, 18, 42, 43, 53, 56, 57, 62, 67, 99, 120, 126, 130 • Jay Directo/AFP/Getty Images: 90, 98 • John Borthwick/Lonely Planet Images: 10, 48, 102, 107 • John Elk III/Lonley Planet Images: 34 • John Pennock/Lonely Planet Images: 6, 46, 117 • Kimberley Coole/Lonely Planet Images: 104 • Mark Webster/Lonely Planet Images: 41 • Michael Coyne/Lonely Planet Images: 110 • Noboru Komine/Lonely Planet Images: 114 • Richard I'Anson/Lonely Planet Images: 40, 115, 123 • Romeo Gacad/AFP/Getty Images: 15 • Salingpusa/SXC. hu: 137 • Seong Joon Cho/Lonely Planet Images: 8 • Toledo/AFP/Getty Images: 31 • Tom Cockrem/Lonely Planet Images: 5, 26, 63, 65, 74, 84, 93, 94, 96, 105, 125 • US Signal Corps/Time & Life Pictures/Getty Images: 30 • Veronica Garbutt/Lonely Planet Images: 38, 127

PRECEDING PAGE

Kids in stilt village in San José in Mindoro.

Publisher (U.S.): Michelle Bisson
Writers: Lily Rose R. Tope, Detch P. Nonan-Mercado, Yong Jui Lin
Editors: Deborah Grahame-Smith, Stephanie Pee
Copyreader: Tara Tomczyk
Designers: Nancy Sabato, Darren Tan
Cover picture researcher: Tracey Engel
Picture researcher: Joshua Ang

Marshall Cavendish Benchmark
99 White Plains Road
Tarrytown, NY 10591
Website: www.marshallcavendish.us

© Times Media Private Limited 1990. First Edition.
© Times Media Private Limited 2002. Second Edition.
© Marshall Cavendish International (Asia) Private Limited 2012. Third Edition.
® "Cultures of the World" is a registered trademark of Times Publishing Limited.

Originated and designed by Times Media Private Limited
An imprint of Marshall Cavendish International (Asia) Private Limited
A member of Times Publishing Limited

Marshall Cavendish is a trademark of Times Publishing Limited.

All Internet sites were correct and accurate at the time of printing. All monetary figures in this publication are in U.S. dollars.

Library of Congress Cataloging-in-Publication Data
Tope, Lily Rose R., 1955-
 Philippines / Lily Rose R. Tope, Detch P. Nonan-Mercado, Yong Jui Lin. -- 3rd ed.
  p. cm. -- (Cultures of the world)
Includes bibliographical references and index.
 Summary: "Provides comprehensive information on the geography, history, wildlife, governmental structure, economy, cultural diversity, peoples, religion, and culture of the Philippines"--Provided by publisher.
 ISBN 978-1-60870-993-9 (print) -- ISBN 978-0-7614-0000-4 (ebook)
 1. Philippines--Juvenile literature. I. Nonan-Mercado, Detch P. II. Yong, Jui Lin. III. Title. IV. Series: Cultures of the world (3rd ed.)

DS655.T66 2013
959.9--dc23   2011042594

Printed in Malaysia
7 6 5 4 3 2 1

CONTENTS

PHILIPPINES TODAY

PHILIPPINES IS AN ARCHIPELAGO COMPRISING 7,107 ISLANDS and is categorized broadly into three main geographical divisions: Luzon, the Visayas, and Mindanao, covering a land area of 115,831 square miles (300,000 square kilometers). To its north across the Luzon Strait lies Taiwan. To its west across the South China Sea sits Vietnam. The Sulu Sea, to the southwest, lies between the country and the island of Borneo, and to the south the Celebes Sea separates it from the other islands of Indonesia. It is bounded on the east by the Philippine Sea. Its location on the Pacific Ring of Fire and its tropical climate make Philippines prone to earthquakes and typhoons but have also endowed the country with natural resources and made it one of the richest areas of biodiversity in the world.

The Philippines is the world's 12th most populous country. Multiple ethnicities and cultures are found throughout the islands. The Philippines is the most populous Christian nation in East Asia, due to its Spanish and then American heritage. Religion has played a central role in the lives of Filipinos, yet, due to the Catholic Church's prohibition on birth control, it has played a central role in the population explosion

The Philippines is one of the most populous countries in the world and its capital city of Manila has one of the highest population densities.

in the Philippines. In the 1970s both the Philippines and Thailand had populations of about 50 million. Now Thailand has a population of 66.7 million and the Philippines has a population of 101 million. GDP per capita is $8,500 in Thailand and $3,300 in the Philippines. Clearly the pie is being sliced very thinly in the Philippines. The current president, Benigno Aquino III, has risked ex-communication from the Church in order to promote long overdue birth control measures in the Philippines.

This population explosion does not augur well for the Philippines environment. The wildlife of the Philippines has a significant number of plant and animal species that are endemic to the Philippines. The Philippines is considered a global biodiversity hotspot. It has the highest rates of discovery in the world, with 16 new species of mammals discovered in the last 10 years. Some of the endemic animals are the adorable Philippine tarsier, the world's smallest primate; the Mindoro; and the Philippine eagle.

The national economy of the Philippines is the 46th largest in the world, with an estimated 2010 gross domestic product (GDP) of $189 billion. Primary exports include semiconductors and electronic products, transport equipment, garments, copper products, petroleum products, coconut oil, and fruits. The Philippines is the world's largest producer of coconuts. After World War II, the country was for a time regarded as the second wealthiest in East Asia, next only to Japan. However, by the 1960s, its economic performance started being overtaken. The economy stagnated under the dictatorship of Ferdinand Marcos, as the regime spawned economic mismanagement and political volatility. The country suffered from slow economic growth and bouts of economic recession. Only in the 1990s with a program of economic liberalization did the economy begin to recover.

The economy is heavily reliant on remittances, which surpass foreign direct investment as a source of foreign currency. Regional development is uneven, with Luzon—Metro Manila in particular—enjoying most of the new economic growth at the expense of the other regions, although the government has taken steps to ensure parity in economic growth by promoting investment in other areas of the country. Despite constraints, service industries such as tourism and business process outsourcing have been identified as areas with some of the best opportunities for growth for the country. Despite enjoying sustained economic growth during the first decade of the 21st century, as of 2010, the country's economy remained smaller than those of its Southeast Asian neighbors—Indonesia, Thailand, Malaysia, and Singapore—in terms of GDP. Estimates show that 32.6 percent of the population is still below the poverty line.

There are 11 million overseas Filipinos—constituting 11 percent of the total population of Philippines. In 2009 about $17.348 billion in remittances was sent to the Philippines by overseas Filipinos. Filipinos are the second-largest Asian-American group in the United States, next only to the Chinese.

Farmers plowing their land in preparation for planting.

The Chocolate Hills of Bohol Island.

As the second-largest archipelago in the world, with more than 7,000 tropical islands, the Philippines is a place of natural wonders—a string of coral-fringed islands strewn across a vast expanse of the western Pacific. Under the sea level, the Philippines boasts of some of the world's best diving and snorkeling, including wreck diving around Coron and swimming with the whale sharks off Donsol. There are plenty of wonders on land as well to keep visitors amazed: the Chocolate Hills of Bohol, Banaue and the Rice Terraces, and fascinating reminders of the islands' history in places such as Samar and Leyte, and Vigan. The Philippines also boasts five United Nations Educational, Scientific and Cultural Organization (UNESCO) World Heritage Sites.

No visit to the Philippines is complete without tasting some of the street food there. Filipinos have their own distinct range of street food. Some of these are skewered on sticks in the manner of a kebab. One such example is *banana-cue* (banana-QUEUE), which is a whole banana or plantain skewered on a short thin bamboo stick, rolled in brown sugar, and fried. *Kamote-cue* (KAH-MOH-TEH-QUEUE) is a peeled sweet potato skewered on a stick, covered with brown sugar, and then fried. Fish balls or squid balls are skewered on bamboo sticks, and then dipped in a sweet or savory sauce to be commonly sold frozen in markets and peddled by street vendors. *Turon* (TWO-rhon), a kind of fried spring roll consisting of an eggroll or phyllo wrapper filled with banana and jackfruit and sprinkled with sugar, can also be seen sold in streets. Street food is also characterized by the vendor's ability to make use of animal parts that are cheap, thus maximizing profit, hence the use of intestines (*isaw*) and chicken feet (*adidas*).

Street foods featuring eggs include *kwek-kwek* (KHWEK-khwek), which is a hard-boiled quail egg dipped in orange-dyed batter and then deep-fried, like tempura. *Tokneneng* (THOCK-neh-neng) is a larger version of *kwek-kwek* using chicken or duck eggs. Another Filipino egg snack is *balut* (BAH-loot), essentially a boiled fertilized poultry egg, usually of a duck or chicken. There is also another egg dish called *penoy* (PEH-noy) that is basically prepared from hard-boiled unfertilized duck eggs.

Okoy (OH-koy) is another batter-covered, deep-fried street food in the Philippines. Along with the batter, it normally includes bean sprouts, shredded pumpkin, and very small shrimps, shells and all. It is commonly dipped in a combination of vinegar and chili. There are also *pinoy* (PEA-noy) fries, which are made from sweet potatoes.

Barbecued chicken parts for sale at a roadside food stall in Lapu Lapu City.

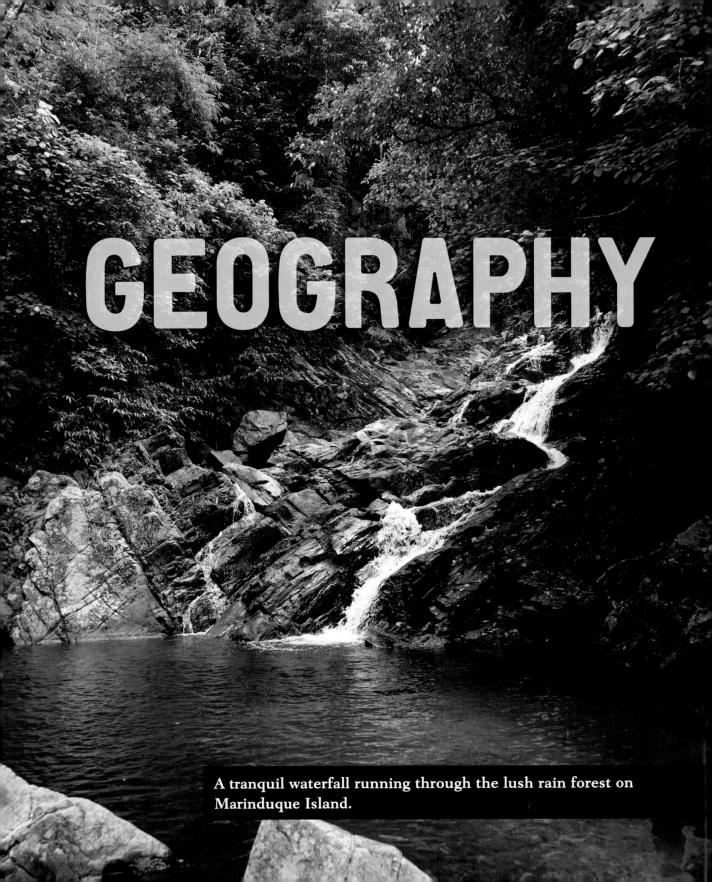

GEOGRAPHY

A tranquil waterfall running through the lush rain forest on Marinduque Island.

1

THE REPUBLIC OF THE PHILIPPINES is an archipelago of 7,107 islands splayed like a necklace in the Western Pacific, separated from mainland Asia by the South China Sea.

In 1751 Father Juan J. Delgado, a Jesuit historian, nicknamed the Philippines "The Pearl of the Orient." Manila's galleon trade then conveyed silk, porcelain, spices, pearls, and other goods from the East to the West.

Reaching toward Taiwan in the north and almost touching Borneo in the south, the Philippine islands occupy a land area of 115,1831 square miles (299,764 square km)—slightly larger than the state of Arizona—and have a combined coastline that is twice the length of that of the

The mist shrouded rain forest of Camiguin Island in the Babuyan Islands.

Limstone rock formations line the white sand beach in Bacuit Bay.

United States. Less than a third of the islands are inhabited, and the largest 11 account for 95 percent of the total land area. Mountain ranges running through the island chain contrast with the green lower slopes and coastal plains.

LUZON, THE VISAYAS, AND MINDANAO

The Philippines can roughly be divided into three main islands: Luzon, the Visayas, and Mindanao. Luzon, the largest island in the Philippine archipelago, is also the most populated. It includes Metro Manila, which is home to 20 million Filipinos (including its suburbs), and one of the world's best harbors, Manila Bay. With its strategic marine location, Manila is the most logical seat of national government and commerce.

South of Luzon is a network of islands collectively called the Visayas. The most important Visayan islands are Leyte, Negros, Samar, Panay, and Cebu. Cebu is the region's business and industrial center. In 1565 explorer Miguel López de Legaspi established the first Spanish colony in the Philippines in Cebu. In 1571 he moved the colonial base to Manila, which then became the seat of power and business for the next four centuries.

Mindanao has a healthy economy based on trade and industry, although parts of the island still lag behind Luzon and the Visayas because of poor communication links and technological infrastructure. The wide use of mobile phones and the popularity of short messaging service (SMS), known locally as mobile phone texting, has brought Mindanao residents closer to their neighbors in Cebu and Manila, the country's largest urban centers. Through SMS, Filipinos throughout Mindanao are sharing ideas and sometimes even carrying out business.

Mount Mayon, the Philippines' most active volcano, rises 8,000 feet (2,438 meters) into the sky over southeastern Luzon. The name Mayon comes from the Bicol word magayon, *meaning "beautiful." (Bicol is a region made up of six provinces: Albay, Camarines Norte, Camarines Sur, Catanduanes, Masbate, and Sorsogon.) Mount Mayon still has a beautiful, almost perfect conical shape, even after at least 49 eruptions over the last 395 years. Despite the obvious danger, farmers cultivate rice up to 5 miles (8 km) from the volcano.*

The first recorded Mayon eruption was in 1616. The most devastating eruption occurred in 1814, burying nearby towns in mudflow and ash and claiming more than 2,000 lives. Only the bell of the church tower remains as a reminder of Mayon's wrath. The volcano unleashed its fury in February 2000, displacing some 80,000 people. Its 48th major eruption was a quiet effusion of lava on July 14, 2006, which was aggravated when a lahar (a mudflow brought about by a volcanic eruption) caused by the rains of Typhoon Durian that followed on November 30, 2006. A 49th summit eruption occurred on August 10, 2008.

LAND OF FIRE AND HEAVING EARTH

The geological birth of the Philippine archipelago was the result of volcanic activity and the movement of the tectonic plates. These processes led to the formation of islands, mountains, and oceanic trenches in many parts of the world, but few events were this dramatic. In the case of much of the Philippine archipelago, coral, which thrives in the warm waters where the islands lie, accumulated in ancient times to form the foundations of the islands.

An aerial view of Mount Pinatubo, a dormant volcano.

There is a popular theory that during the Ice Age, land bridges connected the Philippine islands to other islands in the region and to the Asian continent and that these bridges provided a path for the spread of terrestrial wildlife. If this theory is presumed correct, there are similarities in flora and fauna found in the Philippines and in Sulawesi (Celebes), the Moluccas, Borneo, and even Taiwan, although these countries are now separated by large bodies of water.

Although nature has blessed the Philippines with abundant natural resources, it has also cursed the country with a sometimes dangerous and unpredictable environment. The Philippines lies in a zone of earth fractures around the Pacific Ocean that is prone to earthquakes. The archipelago also forms a link in a volcanic belt known as the Pacific "Ring of Fire," which coincides with the edges of the Pacific plate, where more than half of the world's active above-sea-level volcanoes lie.

The Philippines experiences one large-magnitude (7.75 or higher on the Richter scale) tectonic earthquake every 10 years, seven earthquakes of major magnitude (7.0 to 7.4) every 10 years, and five earthquakes of moderate magnitude (6.0 to 6.9) every year. There are some 21 active volcanoes spread across the Philippine archipelago; the major ones are Mayon, Taal, Hibok-Hibok, and Kanlaon.

Although volcanic eruptions have caused extensive damage in the country, they have also been responsible for the superior quality of Philippine soil. In addition, volcanoes are an excellent source of thermal energy. The Philippines is the world's second-biggest geothermal producer behind the United States, with 18 percent of the country's electricity needs being met by geothermal power.

The Philippine Institute of Volcanology and Seismology studies earthquakes and volcanic activity in the Philippines, gathering information to help predict earthquakes and eruptions and avert the potentially disastrous results.

In 1991, together with the U.S. Geological Survey (USGS), the institute successfully forecast the Mount Pinatubo eruption. The timely evacuation of people living near the volcano saved thousands of lives.

A power station in Cullat Village in Albay province destroyed by volcanic debris that was triggered by a typhoon in 2006.

CLIMATE

The Philippines is generally warm and wet, with temperatures ranging from 77°F to 100°F (25°C to 37°C) and an average annual rainfall of 80 inches (203 centimeters). The Philippines has a tropical maritime climate and is usually hot and humid. There are three seasons: *tag-init* or *tag-araw*, the hot dry season or summer from March to May; *tag-ulan*, the rainy season from June to November; and *tag-lamig*, the cool dry season from December to February. The southwest monsoon (from May to October) is known as the Habagat, and the dry winds of the northeast monsoon (from November to April), the Amihan. The average annual temperature of Baguio at an elevation of 4,900 feet (1,500 m) above sea level is 18.3°C (64.9°F), making it a popular destination during the hot summers. Likewise, Tagaytay is a favored retreat.

TYPHOONS The typhoon is a strong tropical cyclone equivalent to the hurricane in North and Central America. Typhoons are characterized by air spinning violently in a counter-clockwise direction and a calm core called the "eye." Typhoons often travel in a slightly curved path as they pass over land, but they are also known to turn back, not only once but several times, or to mysteriously tarry.

Typhoons are categorized into four types according to their wind speeds by the Philippine Atmospheric, Geophysical, and Astronomical Services Administration (PAGASA):

Tropical depressions have maximum sustained winds of between 34 miles per hour (55 km per hour) and 40 miles per hour (64 km per hour) near the center. Tropical storms have maximum sustained winds of 40.4 miles per hour (65 km per hour) and 74 miles per hour (119 km per hour). Typhoons achieve maximum sustained winds of 74.6 miles per hour (120 km per hour) to 115 miles per hour (185 km per hour). Super typhoons have maximum winds exceeding 115 miles per hour (185 km per hour).

Elementary school classes are canceled when tropical depressions are expected. Intermediate and high school classes are cancelled when tropical

The most active season, since 1945, for tropical cyclone strikes on the archipelago was 1993, when 19 tropical cyclones moved through the country.

In 2010, Typhoon Megi hit the Philippines with winds of up to 160 miles per hour (257 kilometers per hour).

storms are expected. Expected typhoons result in the cancellation of all classes, and people are supposed to stay indoors. Typhoons occur in the months of the southwest monsoon, often bringing heavy rains, floods, and even gigantic waves as they hit land. In a typical year, 21 typhoons strike the Philippines, affecting nearly 700,000 people, damaging more than 7,000 buildings, and destroying agricultural crops.

Typhoon Conson was the second tropical cyclone during the 2010 Pacific typhoon season to impact the Philippines. At 11:00 P.M. on July 13, it was forecast that the typhoon would hit Quezon province, Metro Manila, and southern Luzon provinces. However, residents living in these areas were not advised that the typhoon would hit their areas and they also were not informed that a typhoon might hit the area. Severe damage ensued. Later that same day, President Benigno Aquino III reprimanded PAGASA for failing to predict that Conson would pass over Manila.

FLORA

The Philippines is one of the world's richest wildlife havens. With an estimated 13,500 plant species in the country, 3,200 of which are unique to the islands, Philippine rain forests boast an array of flora, including many rare types of orchids and rafflesia. The narra is considered the most important type of hardwood. Of the flowering plants, the orchid family is the largest, with about 940 species, 790 of which are native. The coastal mangrove swamps are also covered with lush plant growth. Unfortunately the rain forests now constitute only 23.9 percent of the country's total land area.

ABACA This plant from the banana family is known as Manila hemp. The stem of the abaca is stripped lengthwise and made into rope and fabric. Foreign seamen in the 19th century discovered the tensile strength of abaca fibers and their ability to withstand the corrosiveness of seawater.

COCONUT The coconut palm is called the tree of life because of its versatility. Humans have found a use for every part of the palm, from its deepest root to

The highest wind velocity for a typhoon that crossed the Philippines was recorded in Virac on November 30, 2006, when Typhoon Reming (Durian) had a peak gust of 198 miles per hour (320 km per hour).

The endangered tarsier is one of the world's smallest primates and is endemic to the Philippines.

its farthest frond—for food and drink, for building roofs and walls, for fuel, and for making products such as jewelry, mattresses, and paper. In colloquial Filipino, the brain is referred to as the coconut, as in the expression "use your coconut."

FAUNA

Around 1,100 land species can be found in the Philippines, including more than 100 mammal species and 170 bird species not thought to exist elsewhere. The endemic species include the tamaraw of Mindoro, the Visayan spotted deer, the Philippine mouse deer, the Visayan warty pig, the Philippine flying lemur, and several species of bats. Some species of animals in the Philippines are similar to those found on other islands in the region, particularly in Borneo and Java. Ancient land bridges enabled the migration of wildlife around Southeast Asia, while traders and conquerors brought foreign species from farther afield to the Philippines. The archipelago has 612 bird species, and its reefs are famous for their size and diverse marine life. Although a considerable number of animal species inhabit the Philippines, each is represented by a small number. One reason may be that there are so many islands forming unique ecosystems.

Unfortunately humans are also responsible for the dwindling numbers of many animal species in the Philippines. Many animals known to exist only in the Philippines are now recognized as endangered or threatened. The monkey-eating eagle, the largest of all eagles, is the object of worldwide concern. Declared the national bird of the Philippines in 1995, this eagle is barely surviving deforestation. It is critically endangered, mainly due to massive loss of habitat as a result of deforestation in most of its range. Killing a Philippine eagle is punishable under Philippine law by 12 years in jail and heavy fines. Other birds and animals in danger of extinction are a deep-forest bird called Koch's Pitta, the mouse deer, the pelican, the Sarus crane, and the nocturnal tarsier, one the smallest primates. The Philippine tarsier is not a large animal; it measures only about 3.35 to 6.30 inches (85 to 160 millimeters) in height, making it one of the smallest primates on earth. Due to the rapidly growing human population, which causes more and more forests to be converted to farmland, housing areas, and roads, the places where the Philippine tarsier can live its secluded life are disappearing.

Certain animals support human activity directly and substantially. To Filipino peasants, the most important animal is the carabao, or water buffalo. Capable of backbreaking work and being very patient, the carabao is the symbol of Filipino industriousness and perseverance. The smaller and wilder cousin of the carabao, the tamaraw, can be found only on the island of Mindoro.

METRO MANILA

One of the biggest and most modern city networks in Asia, Metropolitan Manila, or simply Metro Manila, is a metropolis of 16 cities. It has a population of 23.96 million—nearly 24 million. Metro Manila is the most populous of the 12 defined metropolitan areas in the Philippines and the 11th most populous in the world.

The old city of Manila was for centuries the nation's capital. However, in 1937, the president, Manuel Quezon, perhaps alarmed at the crowding in Manila and rising crime rate, decided to create a new capital in spacious, suburban Quezon. Quezon was officially the capital of the Philippines from 1948 to 1976. But Manila's historical importance could not be ignored. In 1976 Manila regained its former status as the nation's capital.

Makati is the nation's business center. The most important towns in Metro Manila are Alabang, Novaliches, and Valenzuela—all industrial towns. Metro Manila is a place of economic extremes. Many high-income citizens are concentrated in gated communities in places such as Forbes Park, or in high-rise developments in or around central business districts, such as Rockwell Center in Makati.

The Makati City skyline.

In sharp contrast to these residences are the slums and illegal settlements scattered across the metropolitan area, often found on vacant government land or in districts such as Tondo.

MINDANAO

The Philippine government's decades-long confrontation with Muslim separatists on the southern island of Mindanao and a second conflict with communist insurgents across the country have left some 160,000 dead and displaced more than 2 million people. The Mindanao conflict first flared in the 1960s when the Muslim minority—known as the Moros—launched an armed struggle for their ancestral homeland in the south. Fighting escalated in 2008 after a decade-long peace process between the government and rebel Moro Islamic Liberation Front (MILF) collapsed. The two sides signed a truce in July 2009. The Moro National Liberation Front (MNLF) is another Islamic nationalist political organization that was founded by Nur Misuari in 1969. The MNLF struggles against the Philippine government to achieve independence of the Bangsamoro Land (or Bangsamoro Nation). As defined by the MNLF, the territory of Bangsamoro Land covers Sulu, Mindanao, and Palawan.

The campaign for self-rule is not the only source of bloodshed on Mindanao. There has also been violence linked to militant Islamist groups with pan-Asian aspirations, bloody ethnic vendettas, clan wars, and banditry. Politics and religion aside, much of the violence is fueled by deep poverty rooted in decades of under-investment. Due to these instabilities, travelers are advised to avoid going to Mindanao.

HISTORIC MANILA

Legend has it that Manila, known in early times as *Maynilad* (My-NEE-lahd), was named after the *nilad* (NEE-lahd) plant floating on the Pasig

River. Blessed with a fine harbor, Manila attracted explorers, traders, and settlers. It was already a thriving community when Miguel López de Legaspi arrived in the 1560s. He built turreted walls 33 feet (10 m) thick around the city and turned it into a fortress surrounded by moats. He called the city Intramuros, meaning "within the walls." During the Spanish colonial period, only the Spaniards were allowed to live within the walled city of Intramuros.

Except for British rule for two years, the walled city was the Spanish empire's political, commercial, and cultural center in the East. When the Americans arrived in 1898, the city had outgrown its walls, leaving Intramuros as a mere district.

Manila is the traditional seat of political power. Colonial governors and Philippine presidents have resided in the Malacañang Palace by the Pasig River. Significant events have taken place in Manila, such as the execution in 1896 of José Rizal; the birth of the Philippine Republic in 1948; and more recently the rise of "people power," which replaced Ferdinand Marcos with Corazon Aquino as president and later Joseph Estrada with Gloria Arroyo.

Manila has had its share of natural and historical catastrophes. In fact, during World War II, it was the world's most devastated city after Warsaw, Poland. Despite these events, Manila has survived and persisted. Like old wine, it has acquired more flavor with the passage of time.

MAJOR CITIES

MANILA Manila is a truly teeming metropolis that is getting bigger each day, both in population, with people pouring in from the hinterlands, and size, as new developments in all directions swallow up villages and rice fields. Take in the pulse of the world's most densely populated city here.

CEBU Known as the Queen City of the South, Cebu is the most important city in the Visayas and the regional center of commercial and intellectual activity. Cebu city is the capital of Cebu province, whose soil is not good for farming, but perfect for industrial development. The city of Cebu is the second most significant metropolitan center in the Philippines and is known as the oldest settlement established by the Spaniards in the country. Cebu is the Philippines' main domestic shipping port and is home to about 80 percent of the country's domestic shipping companies. Cebu also has the second-largest airport for international flights in the Philippines and is a significant center of commerce, trade, and industry in the Visayas and Mindanao regions.

On the nearby island of Mactan, Ferdinand Magellan was defeated in battle in 1521 by a local chieftain named Lapu-Lapu. A large wooden cross left by Magellan in 1521 now stands in a plaza in commemoration of the Spanish arrival.

DAVAO Davao is the largest city in Mindanao and the largest city in the Philippines outside Metro Manila. It is also the richest city in the country outside Metro Manila. The early Davao inhabitants were the Manobo, famous for their colorful costumes and musical instruments. In recent years Davao City has emerged as the business, investment, and tourism hub for

Children in an innovative Caraboa-drawn sled in Davao.

the entire southern Philippines. The city has good beaches and mountain resorts, and is close to diving spots and the highest peak in the Philippines, Mount Apo. It was awarded the title of "Most Livable City in the Philippines" in 2008 by the Department of Tourism. The stable banana and flourishing pineapple industries are among the country's leading export commodities. A net exporter since 1987, Davao City largely contributed to making the Philippines the world's top exporter of papaya and mangosteen.

BAGUIO The city of Baguio is at an altitude of approximately 5,100 feet (1,500 m) in the Luzon tropical pine forests eco-region, conducive to the growth of mossy plants and orchids. It is the highest major Philippine city in terms of elevation. It is because of this that Baguio is nicknamed the "Summer Capital of the Philippines." Baguio rests on a 4,900-foot (1,494-m) plateau in the Cordillera Mountains. Owing to its high elevation, the temperature in the city is 46.4°F (8°C) lower compared with the average temperature of the rest of the country. The temperature in Baguio seldom exceeds 78.8°F (26°C) even during the warmest part of the year.

INTERNET LINKS

www.philippines.hvu.nl/animals1.htm

This engaging website contains attractive pictures about the animals in the Philippines.

www.philippines.hvu.nl/volcanoes1.htm

An interesting website on the volcanoes of the Philippines.

www.weather.gov.ph/

This fascinating website by the Philippines weather service (Philippine Atmospheric, Geophysical, and Astronomical Services Administration) includes storm warnings and downloadable weather forecasts.

HISTORY

The Cagsawa Ruins are the remnants of an 18th-century Franciscan church that was built in 1724 in Barangay.

2

The history of the Philippines can be divided into four distinct phases: the pre-Spanish period (before 1521); the Spanish period (1521–1898); the American period (1898–1946); and the post-independence period (1946–present).

THE AETA, OR NEGRITO, ARE thought to be the earliest inhabitants of the Philippines. More recent theories propose that this small-built, dark-skinned, curly-haired people migrated to the islands from Southeast Asia more than 22,000 years ago by way of land bridges.

Artifacts discovered in areas populated by Aeta communities in the Philippines indicate that the Aeta initially lived in the lowlands. One theory proposes the later arrival of peoples of Malay origin, who pushed the Aeta into the hills and mountains. The newer immigrants established communities along the sea and rivers. Before long they developed a lifestyle all their own.

Early records indicate the existence of an advanced civilization sustained by rice culture, fishing, mining, weaving, and trading before the Spanish arrival in the Philippines.

The Pre-Spanish Filipinos organized themselves in kinship-based communities called *barangay* (ba-RUNG-gai), the name of the seaworthy vessel on which they traveled to the islands. They followed laws, were governed by a council of elders, and worshiped their ancestors as well as the natural forces around them. They used a form of Indic writing inscribed on bamboo and a shell currency to trade.

The influence of foreign traders enriched indigenous lifestyles. From the Chinese, the early Filipinos acquired the use of porcelain and culinary tools and learned new methods of agriculture. The Indians enriched their language and script. The Arabs brought Islam, which took root in southern Mindanao.

Despite their cosmopolitan exposure, however, the pre-Spanish Filipinos had petty kinship rivalries that divided them. The Spaniards could not have chosen an easier people to colonize.

THE SPANISH CROSS AND SWORD FOR GOD AND GOLD

In search of another route to the Spice Islands, Ferdinand Magellan sailed for the unknown Indies and landed in the Philippines on March 16, 1521. Accompanied by priests, he set up a colony and converted the local chieftains and their families to Christianity.

Five years later, the Spaniards launched a more determined expedition, headed by Miguel López de Legaspi. Equipped with his experience as a conquistador and official in Mexico, Legaspi succeeded in establishing a strong foothold in Luzon and the Visayas. He named the islands "the Philippines" in honor of King Philip II of Spain. Legaspi defeated the petty chieftains and rewarded those who participated in the Spanish conquests with vast tracts of land, huge estates that would later be the workplace of

The San Pedro Fort in Cebu City was built by the Spanish to repel Muslim raiders in 1738.

JOSÉ RIZAL

Born on June 19, 1861, in Calamba, Laguna, José Rizal was a man of extraordinary talent and genius. A medical doctor by training, he was also a poet, musician, architect, scientist, businessman, and more. He spoke several languages, including English, Spanish, Tagalog, and Chinese. His mother, Teodora Alonso, was a great influence in his life. Her imprisonment by the Spanish authorities based on a false accusation kindled in Rizal's young heart anger against all forms of injustice. He also advocated reforms in the Spanish government.

Rizal wrote two novels that exposed the abuses of the Spanish government and clergy: Noli me Tangere *(Touch Me Not), published in English as* The Lost Eden, *and* El Filibusterismo *(The Reign of Greed), published in English as* The Subversives. *On December 30, 1896, he was arrested and publicly executed by a firing squad in Manila, after being found guilty of inciting a Katipunan insurrection that he had had no connection with. His name became the battle cry in the fight for independence.*

indigenous farmers and provide the Spaniards with comfortable living and prominent social status.

Spain ruled the Philippines via Mexico. Huge bulky ships called galleons plied between Manila and Acapulco loaded with silk, porcelain, gold, and spices bound for Europe, bringing unmeasured prosperity to investors.

The Spaniards' position in the islands was strengthened by the priests who, convinced they had to save the islands' pagan souls, embarked on a rigorous and sometimes brutal conversion campaign, baptizing the majority of the lowlanders within a short time. Social activities in the towns centered on churches built by the friars, who equaled and often surpassed the civil government in influence and power. Church and state remained entangled in the Philippines for three centuries. The Spaniards were hard taskmasters. They imposed forced labor on the indigenous people, derogatorily calling them Indios, and demanded unreasonable tributes from them. Even the clergy were known to be abusive.

In 1571 the Spanish established Manila as the capital of the Spanish East Indies.

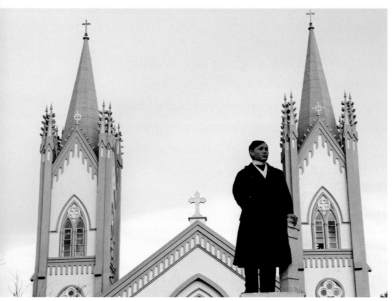

Statue of Dr. José Rizal in front of the Immaculate Conception Cathedral in Palawan.

Meek as they were, the Indios were often pushed to revolt but were easily quelled by the Spaniards' superior arms and "divide-and-rule" tactics. It was not until the 1800s that some form of sustained movement for social and political freedom was started. With the rise of a middle class, the sons of rich families acquired a European education and, consequently, liberal ideas. They worked to bring about reforms and held strong anti-clerical views. Among them, José Rizal stood out, with his non-violent, reformist approach. His arrest and execution in 1896 fueled the fires of a revolution led by Andres Bonifacio, the founder of a secret anti-Spanish organization called Katipunan, or Brotherhood. Bonifacio was killed by another rival anti-Spanish faction, and he was replaced by Emilio Aguinaldo. On June 12, 1898, the first Philippine Republic was proclaimed.

THE AMERICAN ADVENTURE

The republic was short-lived, and rebel leader Aguinaldo was exiled. In the meantime, the Spanish-American War broke out. In 1898 U.S. Commodore George Dewey sailed into Manila Bay and destroyed the depleted Spanish naval fleet.

The Philippines sided with the United States, in hopes of gaining independence. But after losing the war, Spain ceded the Philippines to the United States for $20 million. Aguinaldo then proclaimed a republic, which the United States refused to acknowledge. So, in 1899, the Philippines went to war with the United States.

Aguinaldo was captured in 1901 and the Philippine-American War finally ended in 1902, with the lure of education-for-all and economic opportunities

In 1901 a converted cattle ship called Thomas *arrived in the Philippines from the United States, carrying 540 teachers. A smaller group had landed two months earlier to supplement soldiers who had stayed as teachers after their tours of duty. However, the Thomasites were the single largest group of teachers sent to educate and civilize their "little brown brothers." In their first 20 months in the islands, 27 Thomasites died of tropical diseases or were killed by bandits. Yet many stayed permanently and gave their time and talent to the cause of nation-building. The American system of universal education gave Filipino children access to knowledge and spread the English language throughout the Philippines.*

too strong to resist. However, members of the Katipunan society, a Philippine revolutionary society founded by anti-Spanish Filipinos in Manila in 1892, continued to battle the American forces. Resistance continued until June 1913, when the rebel groups against American rule were defeated.

The United States viewed its term in the Philippines as preparation for the country's independence. The Americans introduced U.S. political institutions and processes and opened the Philippine market to the West to build economic self-sufficiency. Most important, classrooms were built to educate Filipinos. Where the Spaniards refused to educate the local people "for their own good," the Americans made education compulsory.

By 1934 the promise of a Commonwealth by 1936 and independence by 1946 had been made to Manuel Quezon, who would later become the first president of the Commonwealth. The transition would have been smooth had the Japanese not intervened.

JAPANESE INVASION AND ITS AFTERMATH

On December 10, 1941, three days after the bombing of Pearl Harbor, Japanese forces landed in the Philippines. The 12,000 Philippine scouts

The MacArthur Landing Memorial is situated in Red Beach, Palo, Leyte. The monument marks the spot where General Douglas MacArthur landed with the American Liberation Forces in October 1944, starting the Battle of Leyte.

and 16,000 U.S. soldiers under General Douglas MacArthur, deprived of reinforcements from the United States following the destruction of Pearl Harbor, could not stop the relentless advance of the Japanese into Manila. MacArthur's forces put up a last line of defense at Bataan and Corregidor. Forced to retreat in 1942, MacArthur pledged, "I shall return," a promise that Filipinos never forgot. He made good on this promise in 1944 when, aided by Filipino resistance fighters, U.S. forces reached the capital and defeated the Japanese in their fiercest battle, which claimed 60,000 lives and almost leveled Manila to the ground. Soon after the war, on July 4, 1946, the Philippines was granted independence, with Manuel Roxas at the helm. Extensive rehabilitation was the top priority, but with an empty treasury, the Philippines had to seek financial help from the United States. Thus began the love-hate economic relationship between the Philippines and the United States, a factor that was to shape Philippine policy in the years to come. There were also rumblings of dissent from peasants clamoring for agrarian justice. Defense secretary—and later president—Ramón Magsaysay distinguished himself by quelling the unrest. His ability

After the Marcos family fled Malacañang Palace, Imelda Marcos was found to have left behind 15 mink coats, 508 gowns, 1,000 handbags, and 1,060 pairs of shoes.

American soldiers firing at a Japanese convoy during the invasion of Leyte.

to identify with the people and his concern for their problems restored public confidence in the government.

POWER TO THE PEOPLE

In 1965 Ferdinand Marcos was elected president. In 1969 he became the first president to be re-elected. An astute statesman, Marcos rallied the people with his vow to make the Filipino great again. But his early achievements were soon eroded by the excesses of his later years in office.

On September 21, 1972, amid nationwide dissent, Marcos declared martial law. He jailed or exiled his opponents, installed media controls, abolished the Congress, force-ratified the 1973 constitution, and established his New Society Movement. Marcos and his wife, Imelda, isolated themselves and depleted the nation's coffers with their extravagant lifestyle.

On August 21, 1983, Benigno Aquino, Marcos's exiled political rival, returned to the Philippines and was assassinated on the airport tarmac. His death sparked widespread protest. In January 1986, Aquino's widow, Corazon, challenged Marcos in a snap election. Minister of Defense Juan Ponce Enrile and Vice Chief of Staff Fidel Ramos defected to Aquino's side on February 22. Millions of people trekked to the military camps to protect the defectors from Marcos's forces. Three days later, Marcos left for a Hawaiian exile. The "people power" revolution demonstrated that change could be achieved through peaceful means.

In 2001 "people power" removed Joseph Estrada from the presidency. Estrada entered politics in 1969, at the height of his movie career. He was

The Philippines' first elected president, Ferdinand Marcos.

Former president of Philippines, Gloria Arroyo.

mayor of San Juan, a Manila suburb, for 16 years. In 1987 he became senator, then vice president in 1992, and president in 1998. Barely three years later, he faced impeachment charges, including bribery, betrayal of public trust, and violation of the constitution. In January 2001 Estrada stepped down after a string of generals and cabinet members abandoned his administration.

Vice President Gloria Macapagal-Arroyo (the daughter of the late president Diosdado Macapagal) was sworn in as Estrada's successor on the day of his departure. Her accession to power was further legitimized by the midterm congressional and local elections held four months later, when her coalition won an overwhelming victory. Arroyo's initial term in office was marked by fractious coalition politics as well as a military mutiny in Manila in July 2003 that led her to declare a month-long nationwide state of rebellion.

She was succeeded by President Benigno Aquino, son of former president Corazon Aquino. Benigno Aquino was declared the winner of the 2010 Philippine elections on June 9, 2010.

Benigno Aquino is the first president of the Philippines to be a bachelor, and he is the second president to be a child of a former president (the first was his predecessor, Gloria Arroyo.)

AQUINO'S PRESIDENCY

NO "WANG-WANG" Aquino is famous for his no "*wang-wang*" policy. *Wang-wang* is Filipino street lingo for blaring sirens. Under President Ferdinand Marcos, a decree was issued allowing the use of *wang-wang* only for the president, vice president, Senate president, House speaker, chief justice, Philippine National Police, Armed Forces of the Philippines, National Bureau of Investigation, Land Transportation Office, Bureau of Fire Protection, and ambulances. However, despite having the privilege of using *wang-wang*, Aquino maintained he would set the example for his no *wang-wang* policy, by not using *wang-wang,* even if it means getting stuck in traffic and being late every now and then.

HOSTAGE CRISIS

The Manila hostage crisis occurred when a dismissed Philippine National Police officer took over a tour bus in Rizal Park, Manila, Philippines, on August 23, 2010. Disgruntled former senior inspector Rolando Mendoza, from the Manila Police District (MPD), hijacked a tour bus carrying 25 people (20 tourists and also a tour guide, all from Hong Kong, and four Filipinos) in an attempt to get his job back. He said that he was summarily dismissed without the opportunity to properly defend himself, and that all he wanted was a fair hearing. Eight of the hostages and Mendoza were killed; many other hostages and bystanders were injured. On September 3, 2010, Aquino took responsibility for everything that happened during the Manila hostage crisis.

INTERNET LINKS

www.infoplease.com/ipa/A0107887.html?pageno=1

This website includes an interesting and detailed history of the Philippines.

www.philippine-history.org/

This website provides a concise and accurate overview of Philippine history.

www.tribo.org/history/ww2.html

This site contains a gripping account of what the first bombing of Manila by the Japanese in World War II was like for residents of Manila, with pictures of the destruction in Manila City.

Arroyo was undersecretary of Trade and Industry during Aquino's term. She was elected senator in 1992 and was reelected in 1995. In 1998 she was elected vice president.

GOVERNMENT

Baguio City Hall.

3

PHILIPPINE DEMOCRACY SUFFERED a setback during the Marcos years. In 1987, during the presidency of Corazon Aquino, the constitution was revised to mandate a presidential system of government with three independent branches: the executive, which administers the government; the legislative, which enacts laws; and the judicial, which enforces justice.

Executive power is vested in the president, who is head of state and commander-in-chief of the armed forces. Assisted by a cabinet, the president serves one six-year term and can approve or veto bills passed by the legislative branch, the Congress. The Congress has two chambers: the Senate (with 24 members popularly elected to serve six-year terms) and the House of Representatives (with 250 members serving three-year terms). The judiciary consists of the Supreme Court (with one chief justice and 14 associate justices appointed by the president) and its lower courts, and the court of appeals (with one presiding justice and 68 associate justices).

LOCAL ADMINISTRATION

The Philippines is divided into three island groups: Luzon, the Visayas, and Mindanao. As of March 2010, these were divided into 17 regions, 80 provinces, 138 cities, 1,496 municipalities, and 42,025 *barangays*. The

There have been attempts to change the government to a federal, unicameral, or parliamentary government since the Ramos administration. However, the Philippines remains governed as a unitary state with the exception of the Autonomous Region in Muslim Mindanao, which is largely free from the national government.

highest local unit is the province, which is run by a governor. Each province consists of several districts, each of which has a representative in the Congress. Each district, in turn, is divided into municipalities. Headed by a mayor, the municipality consists of territories called *barangays*. Each *barangay* is headed by a chairperson.

GRASSROOTS GOVERNANCE

The word *barangay* describes the sea vessels used by the early settlers. Originally it also connoted a kinship group. Each *barangay* was headed by a *datu* (DHAH-to), the most prominent man in the village. He was assisted by a council of elders who saw to it that the people in the community observed the ancient laws.

Historically a *barangay* is a relatively small community of around 50 to 100 families. Upon the arrival of the Spanish, several ancient *barangays* were combined to form towns. Every *barangay* within a town was headed by the *barangay* chief, who formed part of the elite ruling class of the municipalities of the Spanish Philippines.

During Spanish rule, the *barangay* chiefs became the representatives of the civil government on a local level. Today the modern *barangay*, or township, is the basic political unit. The *barangay* government has executive, legislative, and adjudicatory powers defined by the Local Government Code.

A chairperson and seven council members lead the *barangay*. These are elected by the township to a three-year term, and they cannot serve more than three consecutive terms in the same office. They meet with officials of other *barangay* in their municipality in the association of barangay councils.

The *barangay* council plans and implements policies at the township level. It also plans development programs according to the needs of the township, mobilizes participation in national and local programs, and evaluates the implementation of these programs. The *barangay* supports the youth of the township with scholarships for the poor and by encouraging civic

President of the Philippines Benigno Aquino took office on June 30, 2010.

association membership, where the youth receive instruction in useful trades to help them earn a living.

SPRATLY ISLANDS

Currently the government of the Philippines is engaged in a dispute with the Chinese government over the Spratly Islands in the South China Sea. In 2005 a cellular phone base station was erected by the Philippines' Smart Communications Company on Pagasa Island.

On May 18, 2011, China Mobile announced that its mobile phone coverage has expanded to the Spratly Islands, under the rationale that it can allow soldiers stationed on the islands, fishermen, and merchant vessels within the area to use mobile services, and can also provide assistance during storms and sea rescues. The deployment of China Mobile's support over the islands took roughly one year to fulfill. The United States has thrown its support behind the Philippines' claim to the highly contested Spratly Islands.

INTERNET LINKS

www.gov.ph/

This is the official website of the government of the Philippines, where press releases and historical papers and documents are published and archived.

www.mongabay.com/reference/country_studies/philippines/ GOVERNMENT.html

This site provides a fair overview of President Corazon Aquino's years in office.

www.traveldocs.com/ph/govern.htm

This site contains a concise summary of the challenges facing the government of the Philippines today.

Under President Corazon Aquino, provision was made in the constitution for autonomous regions in Muslim areas of Mindanao and in the Cordillera region of northern Luzon, where many aboriginal tribes still live.

ECONOMY

A fisherman pulling out his nets at a fish farm on the Gulf of Davao.

4

THE ECONOMY OF THE PHILIPPINES is the 12th-largest economy in Asia, the 32nd-largest economy in the world, and the fourth-largest economy in Southeast Asia.

A newly industrialized emerging market economy, the Philippine economy grew by 7.6 percent in 2010, which several reports described as the fastest growth in 34 years.

Important sectors of Philippine industry include food processing, textiles and garments, and electronics assembly. Most industries are concentrated in the urban areas around Metro Manila, while Metro Cebu is also becoming an attraction for foreign and local investors. Mining also has great potential in the Philippines, which possesses significant reserves of chromite, nickel, and copper. As of 2008 the Philippines was reported to be ranked as one of the five most mineral-rich countries in the world. Recent natural gas finds off the islands of Palawan add to the country's geothermal, hydro, coal, and oil exploration energy reserves.

Annual GDP growth averaged 4.6 percent over the past decade, but it will take a higher, sustained economic growth path—at least 7 to 8 percent per year by most estimates—to make progress in alleviating poverty, given the Philippines' annual population growth rate of 2.04 percent, one of the highest in Asia. The portion of the population living below the national poverty line increased from 24.9 percent to 26.5 percent between 2003 and 2009, equivalent to an additional 3.3 million poor Filipinos.

According to Goldman Sachs, the Philippine economy will become the 14th-largest economy in the world by 2050.

An Ifugo woman transplanting rice saplings.

ECONOMIC SECTORS

Agriculture in the Philippines is a major economic sector, contributing 13.9 percent of the gross domestic product (GDP) and employing 33 percent of the labor force. The country's soil, enriched by volcanic ash, supports a wide range of crops, such as rice, corn, sugarcane, bananas, pineapples, and coconuts.

FISHING AND FISHERIES Coastal and inland waters, with 2,300 species of fish, make good fishing grounds. Fisheries production in the Philippines has grown at an average rate of about 7 percent a year since 2002 due to a large increase in aquaculture output. The Philippines now ranks eighth in the world among leading fishing countries, and has a total annual production of around 5.18 million short tons (4.7 million metric tons) of fishery products, including seaweed. Marine fisheries have an annual growth rate of 6 percent in terms of value. Currently 50 percent of the production is from aquaculture, and 50 percent is from marine catch, raising hopes that the pressure on overfished marine stocks through the Philippines archipelago can be reduced.

In December 2010 AOL's finance site, Daily Finance, proclaimed the Philippine Stock Exchange as the year's best-performing stock market in the world.

Coral reefs are not only important to the ecology of the Philippines, but its economy, too.

The total territorial water area of the Philippines covers 849,425 square miles (2.2 million square km) of which 102,703 square miles (266,000 square km) are coastal waters and 733,594 square miles (1.9 million square km) are oceanic. Not surprisingly the benefits derived from the coastal ecosystem are substantial. Coral reefs alone are estimated to contribute at least $1 billion annually to the domestic economy. Fisheries are an important source of employment in the Philippines, with about 1.6 million people engaged in fishing and related activities, accounting for about 5 percent of the labor force.

Fish consumption has risen in both rural and urban areas in recent years as the volume of fish production has grown each year. Fish is extremely important in the countryside, where sardines and rice make up the staple diet for many people. Canned sardine prices are a political issue in the Philippines due to their importance in the staple diet of low-income families. With canned sardine retail prices now more affordable due to a fall in tinplate prices, the government is taking steps to ensure that improved sardine supplies are available for canning.

The Philippines is the largest producer of tilapia in the world.

CATTLE RAISING

Cattle raising in the Philippines is predominantly a backyard endeavor. They are either stall-fed or tethered along roadsides and backyards and fed with whatever available feed there is. Concentrate feeding is minimal and inputs for health maintenance are generally lacking. Commercial ranches engaged in cattle raising are steadily decreasing in number. This is largely due to a combination of factors such as land use conversion and increasing input costs.

Large-scale cattle raising in the Philippines has been steadily declining.

INDUSTRIES IN THE PHILIPPINES

AUTOMOTIVE The anti-lock braking systems (ABS) used in Mercedes-Benz, BMW, and Volvo cars are made in the Philippines. Ford, Toyota, Mitsubishi, and Nissan are the most prominent automakers manufacturing cars in the country.

ELECTRONICS Intel has been in the Philippines for 28 years as a major producer of products including the Pentium 4 processor. Texas Instruments' Baguio plant produces all the chips used in Nokia cell phones and 80 percent of chips used in Ericsson cell phones in the world. Until 2005 Toshiba laptops were produced in Santa Rosa, Laguna. Currently the Philippine plant's focus is on the production of hard disk drives. Printer manufacturer Lexmark has a factory in Mactan in the Cebu region.

MINING AND NATURAL RESOURCES The country is rich with mineral and geothermal energy resources. In 2003 it produced 1931 megawatts (MW) of electricity from geothermal sources, second only to the United States, and a recent discovery of natural gas reserves in the Malampaya oil fields off the island of Palawan is already being used to generate electricity in three gas-powered plants. Philippine gold, nickel, copper, and chromite deposits are among the largest in the world. Other important minerals include silver, coal, gypsum, and sulfur. Significant deposits of clay, limestone, marble, silica, and phosphate exist. About 60 percent of total mining production is accounted for by non-metallic minerals.

BUSINESS PROCESS OUTSOURCING The Philippines' business process outsourcing (BPO) industry currently accounts for about 15 percent of the global outsourcing market and has been the fastest-growing segment of the Philippine economy. BPO revenues rose 26 percent to nearly $9 billion in 2010. The sector created about 100,000 new jobs in 2010, bringing total BPO employment as of the end of 2010 to about 525,000. As of December 2010 the Philippines had overtaken India as the world leader in business support functions such as shared services and business process outsourcing. The call center industry comprises 80 percent of the outsourcing industry in the country.

A worker in an automotive factory welds together the body of a jeepney at the Saro Jeepney Factory in Luzon.

CALL CENTER INDUSTRY The call center industry is an up-and-coming industry in the Philippines. Call centers have industrial capabilities for almost all types of customer relations, ranging from travel services to technical support, education, customer care, financial services, and customer support.

LEGAL AND MEDICAL TRANSCRIPTION This is a service in which the transcriptionist converts a voice-recorded report into a text format. The Philippines has recently attracted increased amounts of medical transcription outsourcing from the United States due to the fact that English is one of the official languages used in all government transactions in the country and the high literacy in the English language and perhaps, the capability of the average Filipino to understand American idioms, colloquialism, and slang used in medical transcription.

FINANCE, LOGISTICS, AND ACCOUNTING The Philippines is becoming a regional and global hub for shared corporate back-office operations, especially for financial services such as accounting and bookkeeping, account maintenance, and credit card administration.

SOFTWARE DEVELOPMENT AND ANIMATION Fueling the recent growth spurt in the outsourcing industry in the Philippines are more higher-end outsourcing services such as Web design, software development, and animation.

Major studios such as Disney, Marvel, Warner Brothers, and Hanna Barbera have offices in the Philippines. Some of the latest works of Filipino animators include scenes in Pixar's *Finding Nemo*, Paramount Picture's *Barnyard*, and Twentieth Century Fox's *Anastasia*.

INTERNATIONAL TRADE

Besides the United States, the Philippines' other main trading partners are Japan, the Netherlands, Singapore, Hong Kong, China, Germany, and South Korea.

Trade with the United States includes exports of semiconductor devices and computer peripherals, automobile parts, electric machinery, textiles and garments, wheat and animal feeds, and coconut oil. Imports include raw and semi-processed materials for the manufacture of semiconductors, electronics and electrical machinery, transport equipment, cereals and cereal preparations.

The Philippines is ranked among the largest beneficiaries of the Generalized System of Preferences (GSP) program for developing countries,

"The stability of the region will not depend on the military presence of superpowers. It is economic cooperation and a common vision of what the region should be . . . as well as what the condition of the world could be in terms of the reduction of weapons of mass destruction."
—Fidel V. Ramos, the 12th president of the Philippines from 1992 to 1998

A worker loading bananas meant for export onto a ship.

which provides preferential duty-free access to the U.S. market. In 2010 the Philippines was the eighth-largest exporter under the GSP program, with nearly $913 million in duty-free exports to the United States. The Philippines chaired the Association of Southeast Asian Nations (ASEAN) from 2006 to 2007, hosting the ASEAN Heads of State Summit and the ASEAN Regional Forum. The Philippines has played a key role in ASEAN in recent years, ratifying the ASEAN Charter in October 2008. The Philippines is a member of the United Nations (UN) and some of its specialized agencies, and served a two-year term as a member of the UN Security Council (UNSC) from 2004 to 2005, acting as UNSC president in September 2005.

TOURISM

The Philippines' tourism offices around the world promote the country as a tourist destination. Word-of-mouth recommendations from satisfied visitors also help attract tourists, while Filipinos working abroad encourage their friends to visit.

Shopping is one of the things tourists love about the Philippines. The country offers one of world's best bargains. Three of the largest malls in the world are all located in the Philippines.

Recognition of significant attractions by world organizations such as the United Nations Educational, Scientific and Cultural Organization (UNESCO) alerts travelers to must-see sites. For example, in 1992, the UNESCO World Heritage List included four Philippine churches as fine examples of baroque art. The Puerto Princesa Subterranean River National Park, with the longest underground river in the world, was added to the list in 1999.

The rice terraces around Banaue, the Chocolate Hills of Bohol, the port city of Cebu, and thousands of uninhabited islands are other places for tourists to explore.

The Philippines is one of the top three best diving destinations in the world, alongside Palau and the Maldives. The archipelago is one of the top biodiversity hotspots in the world, with the most number of species concentrated in one area. The island of Palawan is home to the spectacular Tubbataha Reef and the breathtaking Puerto Princesa Subterranean River National Park, both UNESCO World Heritage sites.

The rice terraces of Banaue are included on the UNESCO World Heritage list.

The challenge in promoting tourism to nature sites is to protect the environment from possible damage caused by tourism.

UNESCO SITES IN THE PHILIPPINES

BAROQUE CHURCHES Four baroque-styled churches in the Philippines are found on the UNESCO World Heritage List—San Agustin Church in Manila, La Asuncion de la Nuestra Senora in Ilocos Sur, San Agustin Church in Ilocos Norte, and Santo Tomas de Villanueva Church in Iloilo.

The baroque churches have withstood the test of time, surviving earthquakes, typhoons, and even World War II. These churches were built in the 16th century when the Philippines was under Spanish colonial rule, and were specially built to withstand earthquakes. They reflect the European baroque architectural style and have been preserved ever since.

Today they are still actively used for Catholic rites and rituals. They are also popular churches for weddings.

TUBBATAHA REEF Every traveler, especially those interested in diving, must include Tubbataha Reef Marine Park on the list of places to visit. Located in the Sulu Sea, this is home to more than a thousand species of fish, corals, and other marine life. Aside from being a marine park, Tubbataha is also a bird sanctuary.

RICE TERRACES OF CORDILLERA The rice terraces in Banaue, Cordillera, are a magnificent work of agricultural engineering. The system of agricultural terraces was created by the Ifugaos, a native tribe in the northern part of the Philippines. This marvel of ancient engineering is 5,003 feet (1,525 meters) above sea level. The cold weather adds to the beauty of this site as the terraces are usually blanketed with fog. This has been often called the eighth wonder of the world.

VIGAN CITY Vigan is an island that is separated from the mainland by three bodies of water: the Abra River, the Mestizo River, and the Govantes River. The city is unique in the Philippines because it is one of many extensive surviving Philippine historic cities, dating back to the 16th century. Vigan City is well known for its cobblestone streets and great architectural building designs. Despite the changes due to modern life in the Philippines, this city has preserved its Spanish influence.

PUERTO PRINCESA SUBTERRANEAN RIVER NATIONAL PARK   This river system stretches 31.1 miles (50 km) and is considered the longest navigable underground river system in the world. The Puerto Princesa Subterranean National Park is located in the province of Palawan and features limestone, stalactite, and stalagmite formations.

The Chocolate Hills of Bohol are limestone hills that turn brown during summer.

THE JEEPNEY, DESCENDANT OF THE JEEP

Visitors who ride in a jeepney get a fleeting feel of the Filipino lifestyle. "The king of Philippine roads," the jeepney is an elongated, more colorful, and localized version of the American World War II jeep. Each jeepney can carry 16 passengers comfortably, although it may ferry more in areas where transportation is limited. There are three entrances: two front doors for the driver and two passengers, and one at the back leading to the main passenger area. Flamboyant colors, decorations such as flags and curtains, and blaring stereo music make the jeepney a mini fiesta on wheels. The sides of the jeepney are painted with colorful images of rockets, the planets, or whatever the driver likes. There may be a tiny altar hanging at the top of the windshield or on the rearview mirror. The driver etches the names of his family on the dashboard. A board covered with posters of movie stars separates the driver from the passenger compartment, where standing passengers can keep themselves from falling off the jeepney by holding on to two parallel bars running close to the ceiling.

The second- and third-generation jeepneys have air-conditioning units, and closely resemble a minibus. Electric jeepneys are being test-run in Makati. In response to calls for reduced greenhouse gas emissions and the rise in oil prices, a limited number of these have been deployed. These E-jeepneys or minibuses, under the support of Greenpeace, started plying Manila/Makati City streets on July 1, 2008. The vehicles can be charged by plugging into an electric socket, using power from biodegradable waste. The E-jeepney carries 17 passengers and can run 75 miles (120 km) on an eight-hour charge from an electrical outlet.

HUMAN TRAFFICKING

Human trafficking and the prostitution of children are significant issues in the Philippines, often controlled by organized crime syndicates. Human trafficking in the Philippines is a crime against humanity. The Philippines has the fourth-largest number of prostituted children in the world, and authorities have identified an increase in pedophiles traveling to the Philippines.

There are estimated to be 375,000 women and girls in the sex trade in the Philippines, mostly between the ages of 15 and 20 years, though some are as young as 11 years. An article in the newspaper *Davao Today* reported that, according to experts, the growth of tourism in the Philippines in places such as Cebu and Boracay has given rise to the sexual exploitation of women and children. It is estimated that 300,000 sex tourists from Japan alone visit the Philippines every year.

Foreign pedophiles are a major problem in a country like the Philippines. Some foreign pedophiles are very well connected and have positions in industry and politics. Profile studies of these pedophiles show they come mostly from Europe and are usually well off, married, and with children of their own. Some foreign pedophiles arrange bribes and corrupt practices to get the children out of the country and abuse them in another country. The problem of foreign pedophiles continues to be reported in the press. Foreign pedophiles have operated openly in the Philippines. Government officials have been accused of turning a blind eye to the sex tourism trade because it helps promote tourism in the country.

THE LABOR FORCE

The Philippines has a literacy rate of 93 percent. Yet, unable to sustain steady economic growth, the country cannot generate enough jobs to employ a labor force of 39 million, including the thousands who graduate from universities every year.

Many Filipinos leave home, braving the uncertainties of life in a foreign country, to secure a more stable source of income abroad to support themselves and their families. Filipinos work as doctors, nurses, and engineers in the Middle East and as domestic helpers in Hong Kong, Singapore, and some European cities. Filipino entertainers spice up the nightlife in Japan. Some two million Filipinos work in the Middle East, with nearly a million in Saudi Arabia alone.

The Philippines has a large pool of skilled labor, and a relative proficiency in English makes the Filipinos internationally marketable. Employment prospects in developed countries are bright for skilled workers, professionals, and especially information technology specialists as the knowledge-based economy continues to expand.

CORPORATE CULTURE

Filipinos are cordial at work. While Westerners may prefer to get straight to the point in a business meeting, Filipinos generally enjoy small talk and refreshments before getting down to business. Establishing personal relationships and the right atmosphere for negotiation is a necessary part of

Office buildings in Manila.

doing business in the Philippines. Because of this, deals tend to be made more slowly in the Philippines than in the United States. Filipinos also seek group consensus for decisions.

Filipinos place a lot of value on their self-esteem, or *amor propio* (ah-MOR PRO-pio), and get upset when they are criticized in front of other people. The way to deal with Filipino coworkers is to point out their mistakes in private and close cheerfully by inquiring about the family. In general, to avoid embarrassment, Filipinos do not openly disagree with or turn down another person. They may say "yes" when they really mean "I'll think about it" or even "no." The only way to be sure about an agreement is to get it in writing.

Some offices in the Philippines resemble large, extended households or urban villages, with the boss as the head of the family or the chief. Everyone knows everyone else, and coffee breaks are a time to catch up on the latest office romance or to plan an outing after work. Filipinos also chat on the job, a way of acknowledging the presence of their colleagues, no matter how urgent the task at hand. Teasing superiors is a way of personalizing professional relationships and establishing camaraderie.

INTERNET LINKS

www.economywatch.com/world_economy/philippines/

This site contains concise facts about the Filipino economy.

www.humantrafficking.org/countries/philippines

This is a webpage that provides a comprehensive overview of the human trafficking situation in the Philippines.

www.tourism.gov.ph/Pages/default.aspx

This site includes everything you might want to know about tourism in the Philippines—including destinations and statistics.

ENVIRONMENT

The crystal clear waters surrounding the El Nido Islands in Palawan.

T
HE PHILIPPINES IS ONE OF THE 10 most biologically mega-diverse countries and is at or near the top in terms of biodiversity per unit area.

Around 1,100 land vertebrate species can be found in the Philippines, including more than 100 mammal species and 170 bird species not thought to exist elsewhere. Endemic species include the tamaraw of Mindoro, the Visayan spotted deer, the Philippine mouse deer, the Visayan warty pig, the Philippine flying lemur, and several species of bats.

The Philippines lacks large predators, with the exception of snakes, such as pythons and cobras, and birds of prey, such as the national bird, known as the Philippine eagle. Other native animals include the palm civet cat, the dugong, and the Philippine tarsier associated with Bohol.

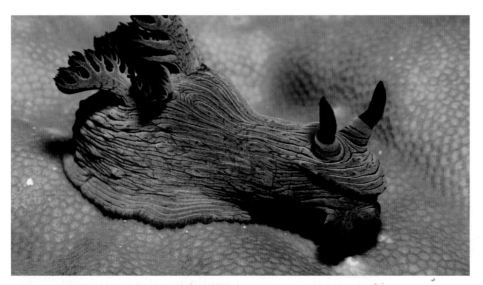

Miller's nembrotha, a species of sea slug, is just one of the strange and wonderful creatures that can be found in the tropical waters off the Philippines.

With an estimated 13,500 plant species in the country, 3,200 of which are unique to the islands, Philippine rain forests boast an array of flora, including many rare types of orchids and rafflesia. The narra is considered the most important type of hardwood.

Philippine maritime waters encompass as much as 850,000 square miles (2.2 million square km) producing unique and diverse marine life and is an important part of the Coral Triangle. There are 2,400 fish species and more than 500 species of coral. The Apo Reef is the country's largest contiguous coral reef system and the second largest in the world. Philippine waters also sustain the cultivation of pearls, crabs, and seaweeds.

Deforestation, often the result of illegal logging, is an acute problem in the Philippines. Forest cover declined from 70 percent of the country's total land area in 1900 to about 24 percent today. Many species are endangered and scientists say that Southeast Asia, of which the Philippines is part, faces a catastrophic extinction rate of 20 percent by the end of the century. The Philippine Department of Environment and Natural Resources (DENR) is the main government body responsible for the conservation, management, and development of the country's natural environment.

According to Conservation International, "the Philippines is one of the few nations that is, in its entirety, both a hotspot and a megadiversity country, placing it among the top priority hotspots for global conservation."

Deforestation, often the result of illegal logging, is a serious problem in the Philippines.

IN DANGER OF EXTINCTION

Among the rare or critically endangered endemic species in the Philippines are the Mindoro dwarf buffalo (tamaraw), the Visayan warty pig, Walden's hornbill, Hazel's forest frog, golden-crowned flying fox, and the Philippine pond turtle.

The dugong, or sea cow, and the Philippine eagle are considered vulnerable species. The dugong, once common throughout the Philippine archipelago, is now believed to inhabit mainly the waters off Palawan. Threats to the survival of the dugong include accidental capture in fishing nets and hunting. Dugong meat used to be sold openly. Although its sale has now been outlawed, there are still illegal vendors of dugong meat. The World Wildlife Fund in the Philippines runs a dugong adoption program to encourage members of the public to pledge financial support for the conservation of this species.

There are fewer than 200 Philippine eagles. Called haring ibon *(HAH-reeng ee-BON) in Tagalog, this eagle stands up to 3.3 feet (1 m) in height and has a wingspan of almost 7 feet (2 m). It feeds on small animals such as lemurs and has an imposing arched bill and a crest of pointed crown feathers. A pair of Philippine eagles can occupy a territory of 23 to 39 square miles (60 to 100 square km). In 2010 the International Union for the Conservation of Nature (IUCN) and BirdLife International listed the Philippine eagle as critically endangered. The IUCN believes that between 180 and 500 Philippine eagles survive in the Philippines.*

GREENING THE ENVIRONMENT

In line with the government's strategy of sustainable development and with the cooperation of many other government agencies, the DENR has implemented forest renewal and rehabilitation projects. Reforestation forms a major part of such projects. The inhabitants in deforested areas plant fast-growing trees—to obtain useful materials such as fuel—and more permanent trees—to protect the land from erosion and flooding. Such programs aim not so much to re-create forests as to help poor communities make a living while rehabilitating the forest.

The government has implemented programs to regenerate, restore, and protect the country's flora by replanting fast-growing trees.

The dugong may have been present around almost all of the islands of the Philippines in the early 1900s. At present sightings of dugongs have been reported in Isabela and Quezon provinces, southern Mindoro and Palawan, Guimaras Strait and Panay Gulf, northeastern Mindanao, and southern Mindanao, including the Sulu Archipelago and Sarangani Bay.

The Philippines has received external support in the form of environmental loans from organizations such as the Asian Development Bank and foreign countries such as Japan to reforest lands that have been denuded by logging and slash-and-burn agriculture.

GUARDING THE COASTS

The 22,548-mile (36,289-km) Philippine coastline is the feeding and breeding ground for fish and marine mammals and reptiles. Reefs bordering the coastline serve as a habitat for some 488 species of coral, 2,000 species of fish, and more than 10,000 invertebrate species.

The Philippines boast 464 reef-building coral species but due to overfishing, destructive fishing techniques, and rapid coastal development in recent years, these reefs have suffered a heavy decline in health. As a response, many Marine Protected Areas (MPAs) have been springing up over the last 20 years, with current estimates at about 600 MPAs. Two examples of MPAs in the Philippines are the Tubbataha National Marine

Park and Mabini Municipal Marine Reserve in Batangas. These MPAs form part of a global network of protected marine areas that includes Australia's Great Barrier Reef.

The Philippines is also working with Malaysia to run the Turtle Islands Heritage Protected Area (TIHPA). These islands harbor one of the world's few remaining major nesting grounds for green turtles. This conservation area aims to ensure the survival of sea turtles that nest in nine islands between the two countries. The coral reefs surrounding these islands also host a variety of fish and invertebrate species. Because of this unprecedented initiative, both implementing agencies were awarded the 20th J. Paul Getty Wildlife Conservation Prize in April 1997.

Besides educating the public about protecting the mangroves, the government has also been replanting mangroves.

Philippine waters also support mangroves, mostly in Mindanao. The country's mangrove forests produce 198,416 short tons (180,000 metric tons) of fish annually, and many mangrove areas have been converted to fish ponds for aquaculture. Government-funded, foreign-aided projects have been implemented over the years to monitor the conditions of the country's mangrove habitats. The government involves local communities in protecting and rehabilitating denuded mangrove areas. Residents are allowed to fish and to harvest wood, but they are also taught about the economic and ecological value of mangroves.

For its efforts in attaining sustainable use of natural resources in its surroundings, the community gains stewardship over the mangrove. The government grants a mangrove stewardship certificate for a 25-year period, renewable for another 25 years, during which the community is to take care of the coastal forest and replant mangroves.

Unfortunately one-fourth of the coral species in the Philippines are vulnerable to extinction.

Land is declared a protected area if it is of outstanding biological importance, supporting habitats of rare and endangered species and related ecosystems. (Species are labeled "rare" if they exist in very small numbers—and are thus rarely seen—in highly specialized habitats in one or a few places in the country. Endangered species are those in danger of extinction, those that are unlikely to survive unless the causes of their disappearance are removed.) Here are some protected areas in the Philippines:

MOUNT GUITING-GUITING NATURAL PARK *The island of Guiting-Guiting in Sibuyan, Romblon province, has grasslands, virgin forests, and coral reefs, surrounded by a jagged shoreline. Some animal species are exclusive to the island: the Sibuyan giant moss mouse, Sibuyan pygmy fruit bat, Sibuyan striped shrew rat, and the greater and lesser Sibuyan forest mouse are found nowhere else in the world. The endangered Philippine tube-nosed bat is also found in this park. Dugongs, dolphins, and whales are sighted in the municipal waters as well.*

MOUNT MALINDANG NATURAL PARK *This park in Mindanao, with its waterfalls and dense virgin forests, is home to the Philippine eagle, flying lemur, long-tailed macaque, and tarsier. The ancestral land of the Subanen, an indigenous people, the Mount Malindang Natural Park is also the site of a biodiversity conservation project that involves the community in such activities as resource management, nursery establishment, and cinnamon propagation. The park has 62 percent forest cover.*

MOUNT PULOG NATIONAL PARK *Plant life in the park includes pine and broad-leaved trees, herbaceous and woody plants, ferns, grasses, mosses, and lichens. Animal life includes the threatened Philippine brown deer, northern Luzon giant cloud rat, and Luzon pygmy fruit bat. The Ibaloi, Kankanaey, Kalanguya, and other indigenous groups living in the area consider the mountain a sacred place.*

MOUNT IGLIT-BACO NATIONAL PARK *This park in central Mindoro has the largest population of tamaraw (70 heads), one of the most endangered large mammals in the world and found only in the Philippines. Also found in this ASEAN Natural Heritage Site are the Mindoro imperial pigeon, black-hooded coucal, scarlet-collared flowerpecker, and bleeding heart pigeon. The human inhabitants are the Mangyan.*

EL NIDO-TAYTAY MANAGED RESOURCES PROTECTED AREA *The El Nido-Taytay Managed Resource Protected Area is located on the northwestern tip of the mainland of Palawan. In 1991 the government of the Philippines proclaimed Bacuit Bay as a marine reserve. In 1998 the protected area was expanded to include terrestrial ecosystems and portions of the municipality of Taytay. This area covers 348.7 square miles (903.21 square km). Tourists are encouraged to pay 50 cents a day to offset the costs of maintaining the area. Its sources of pride are its limestone cliffs, beautiful beaches, mangroves, and rolling farmlands. This area is home to 5 types of forests, 3 major marine habitats, 16 species of birds, 6 species of marine mammals, 4 species of endangered marine turtles, 100 species of corals, and 813 species of fish.*

MOUNT ISAROG NATURAL PARK IN CAMARINES SUR, BICOL PROVINCE *This is the highest forested peak in Southern Luzon and is actually an inactive volcano. The park houses at least 143 kinds of birds, 15 of which are endemic to Luzon. Among these is the sub-species of the velvet-fronted nuthatch, which is found here only. Another species endemic to Mount Isarog is the isolated forest frog. The park nurtures 1,300 known species of plants.*

CORON ISLAND IN THE MUNICIPALITY OF CORON *Coron Town lies almost in the middle of the stretch connecting Manila and Puerto Princesa, Palawan. Most of Coron Island is covered by forest over limestone while its coastline is bordered by mangroves and beach forests. There are at least 500 caves in the Island where balinsasayaw (swiftlets) produce edible bird's nests.*

MALAMPAYA SOUND PROTECTED LANDSCAPE AND SEASCAPE IN NORTHWESTERN PALAWAN *This protected area is a watershed with a rich fishing ground called the Sound (the Inner and the Outer). The name Malampaya comes from a Tagbanua word that means "rich in fish." The Inner Sound may have brackish water, but it boasts of being the only place in the Philippines where the Irrawaddy dolphin can be seen. The Outer Sound is home to sea grass, coral ecosystems, and bottle-nose dolphins. Faunal species of national importance also inhabit the place, including the Philippine mallard, Philippine cockatoo, hawksbill turtle, Philippine macaque, Irrawaddy dolphins, and palm civet. The palm civet spends most of its day hidden in the palms of coconut trees, and hence the name.*

MINDING THE MINES

Mineral wealth is another source of Philippine pride. The country has metallic reserves of gold, copper, nickel, silver, and cobalt, and non-metallic reserves of limestone and marble. Although the mining industry has consistently

A gold mine on Mount Diwata bustles with activity.

been a significant source of revenue, it has also been a major threat to the environment. The Philippine Mining Act of 1995 was enacted to tackle the problems of extensive vegetation clearing, soil erosion, and mine waste.

RECLAIMING METRO MANILA

Some 11.5 million people live in Metro Manila, competing for basic services meant to meet the needs of 3 to 4 million. Most people in Metro Manila have come from the provinces to look for the proverbial greener pastures; they are not about to go back, no matter how crowded or polluted Metro Manila gets.

Metro Manila produces 4,409 short tons (4,000 metric tons) of garbage each day. Paper waste accounts for nearly 14 percent of the daily total. Efforts to reduce pollution are one of the metropolis' major public management concerns, especially with the closure of some garbage dump sites in Greater Manila.

To address the problem of air pollution caused by vehicle emissions, the main source of air pollution in Metro Manila, penalties are dealt out to vehicle owners who exceed emission limits.

INTERNET LINKS

www.camperspoint.com/spip.php?article313

This site contains a list of the national parks and protected areas in the Philippines, with amazing pictures.

www.denr.gov.ph

This is the official website of the DENR, with details on its press releases and programs.

www.richard-seaman.com/Travel/Philippines/Wildlife/index.html

This website includes gorgeous photos of the wildlife of the Philippines.

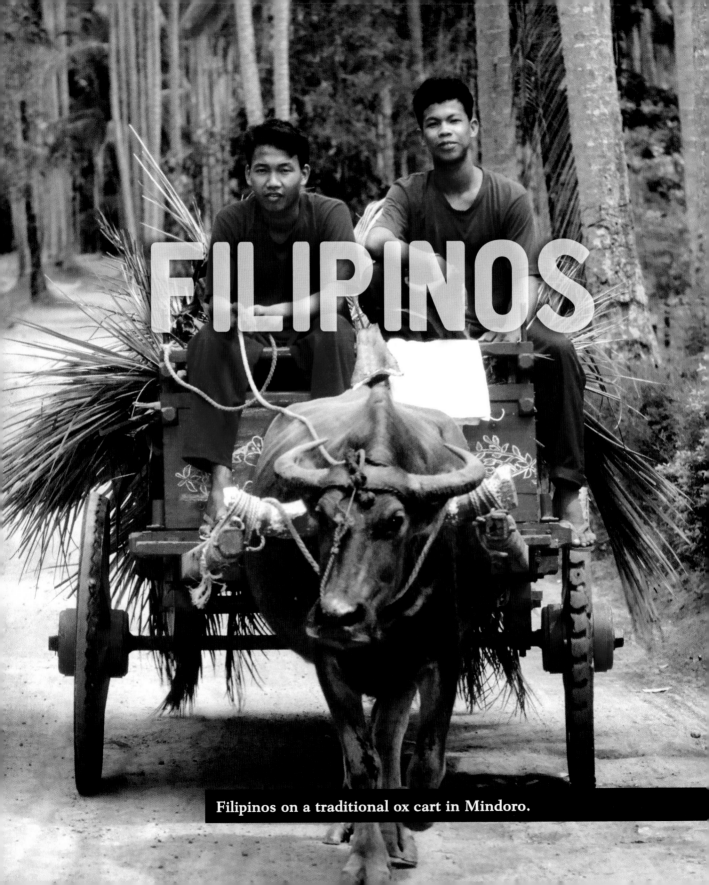

FILIPINOS

Filipinos on a traditional ox cart in Mindoro.

6

T HE PHILIPPINE POPULATION can be divided into three groups: Christians, Muslims, and indigenous animists. These labels are religious distinctions, but they are also indicative of cultural characteristics.

More than 90 percent of Filipinos are Christians. Of these 80 percent belong to the Roman Catholic Church and 10 percent belong to other denominations. The Tagalog live in southern and central Luzon. Visayan-speaking groups predominate in the central Philippines. Migrants from Luzon and the Visayas have established Christian settlements in Mindanao.

It is estimated that 3,000 Filipino babies are born every day; 100,000 every month—rounding up to one million new Filipinos each year.

A group of schoolboys pose for the camera.

Muslim Filipinos, sometimes called Moros, live in Mindanao and the Sulu Archipelago. The Tausug, whose name means "people of the sea current," and the Samal live by the sea, while the Maguindanao, or "people of the flood plain," and the Maranao, meaning "people of the lake," live inland.

The indigenous animists inhabit the less accessible parts of the country. They are the hardy groups of the Cordillera, such as the Ifugao and Kalinga; the shy Aeta in their mountain retreats and seaside coves; the Mindanao hill groups, such as the T'boli, distinguished by their colorful clothing, handicrafts, and rituals; and the gentle Mangyan of the island of Mindoro.

In 1971 it was reported that Stone Age hunter-gatherers had been discovered in the dense rain forests of Cotabato. Skeptics claimed that the community, called Tasaday, was a hoax, although anthropologists who investigated the group confirmed its authenticity.

EMIGRANTS

Apart from the indigenous peoples, few Filipinos can claim pure ethnic descent. Most have inherited Chinese, Indian, Spanish, and Japanese genes from their ancestors.

The Spaniards were free to marry the Indios, though this was not encouraged among the upper classes. Chinese merchants found it convenient to have local wives who could help run their businesses, especially when dealing with local customers. (These merchants usually had families in China but were not allowed to bring them to the Philippines. The same was probably true of the Indian traders.)

The products of this ethnic mixing were the mestizos. The mestizos were initially regarded with disdain or distrust, but the stigma slowly faded, as they proved themselves capable and intermarriages became more common.

THE FILIPINO DRESS

During the Spanish colonial years, upper- and middle-class Filipinos wore cotton skirts and trousers, fine jewelry, and embroidered garments made from *piña*, a transparent fabric woven from the leaf fibers of the pineapple plant.

For added modesty, women wore a triangular scarf-like piece across the bosom. This style of dress is called the Maria Clara, after the heroine in a popular book by José Rizal.

By blending Spanish and indigenous styles of dress, the Filipino elite made a strong fashion statement. They were a new class of Filipinos, educated and prosperous, cultured in the ways of the world. The luxurious clothing and jewelry they wore reflected their status in society and distanced them from the commoners, who were seen as "uncivilized" in their near nakedness.

Modern Filipino dress has evolved through many fashion trends: for women the European ball gown, the tasseled shift of the 1920s, the shoulder pads of the 1940s, the bell-bottoms of the 1960s, and the androgynous look of the 1980s; for men the three-piece suit of the 1920s, the cuffed pants of the 1940s, the leather jackets of the 1960s, and the Wall Street outfit of the 1980s. Today traditional Philippine clothing for men includes the *barong*

A traditionally dressed T'boli man at a festival.

tagalog (BA-rong ta-GA-log), which is made from *piña* or from *jusi* (HU-see) woven from banana tree fibers and worn on formal occasions. Women wear the Maria Clara on special occasions.

THE POLITICS OF FASHION

Clothes, they say, make a statement, and in the Philippines this statement may be as political as it is personal. There have been times in Philippine history when Filipinos wore clothes in shame or defiance, thus giving political color to this usually apolitical aspect of culture.

When some Indios tried to imitate their colonial masters by wearing European coats with tails over tailored trousers, the Spaniards, not wanting to look like the Indios, forbade them from tucking their shirts in!

In the heady days of the "people power" revolution in 1986, Manila was a canvas of political hues: A sea of yellow-clad civilians surrounded two military camps in the capital, their yellow headbands, armbands, and hats indicating

Smokey Mountain has a large squatter community, and it is estimated that 30,000 people live near the site and make their living from picking through the trash at Smokey Mountain.

Supporters of Corazon Aquino at a rally.

their support for Corazon Aquino; a small group clothed in green waved a banner with the name of Vice President Salvador Laurel; the white clothes worn by the seminarians and nuns who braved the tanks; and on the other side of the city, red and blue floated below the balcony where Ferdinand and Imelda Marcos were singing their last duet on Philippine television.

THE UNBALANCED SOCIAL CLASSES

Philippine society has been described as a pyramid: The elite make up the top 0.1 percent of the population. Unfortunately, in the Philippines, the middle class continues to shrink and many people drop into the low-income, non-poor segment of Filipino society (54 percent). The middle class now accounts for 19.1 percent of all the families in the country. A quarter of households (26.9 percent) are considered poor. Enclaves like Forbes Park and Dasmariñas Village, the Philippines' own versions of the United States' Beverly Hills, make it difficult to believe that there are Filipinos living in garbage dumps called Smokey Mountain.

A man picks his way through Smokey Mountain, a large garbage dump.

According to a UN Habitat Report, more than 20 million people in the Philippines live in slums, and in the city of Manila alone, 50 percent of the inhabitants live in slum areas.

Smokey Mountain is a large garbage dump in Manila, Philippines. Consisting of over 2,204,623 short tons (2 million metric tons) of waste, it has operated for over 40 years and is known for decomposing at such high temperatures that it will catch fire, a fact from which the location derives its name. Indeed fires at Smokey Mountain have caused many deaths.

While some houses in Manila have gold bathroom fixtures, children of farmhands die of malnutrition. These contradictions are part of the Philippine landscape and remain a challenge for the nation's leaders.

THE FILIPINA

The modern Filipina (fi-li-PEE-nah) is worlds apart from her ancient ancestor. She is the product of various cultural influences: pre-Spanish self-possession, Castilian medieval morality, American individualism, and Chinese enterprise.

The original Filipina was the priestess who healed illness, exorcised evil, and conveyed spiritual guidance to her community. After the Spanish arrival, a different morality predominated, one that "tamed" women to be demure, gentle, and pious. The effects of the Castilian era are felt even today, as modern Filipinas cling to the Maria Clara ideal. During the last part of the colonization of the Philippines, Isabella II introduced the Education Decree of 1863 that provided for the establishment of at least two free primary schools in each town under the responsibility of the municipal government. That put the Philippines way ahead in offering education for women in Asia, even ahead of some European countries.

An American education taught the Filipina that, like her male partner, she could speak her mind, could excel, and could nurture ambition. Today women outnumber men in universities in the Philippines. They have likewise climbed their way into corporate boardrooms and made their mark in professions previously dominated by men, even running for public office and leading the nation as president.

Filipinas have contributed significantly to nation-building. In the struggle for independence, women acted as keepers of arms, couriers, and social

Gabriela Philippines was founded in April 1984 after 10,000 women marched in Manila, defying a Marcos decree against demonstrations.

covers for their revolutionary relatives. They took care of the wounded, fed the hungry, and sheltered the hunted.

After her husband was assassinated in 1763, Maria Josefa Gabriela Silang took over his rebellion against Spanish rule. Today there is a network of 105 women's organizations named after this famous Filipina. Gabriela Philippines is one of the country's largest assemblies of women and works with the Gabriela Network in America to address international women's issues.

Corazon Aquino is a more recent example, a housewife who became the first woman president of the Philippines, toppling a feared dictator who had said that women were only meant for the bedroom.

The present-day Filipina performs a dual role: the traditional role of homemaker and the modern role of breadwinner. A Filipino mother continues to nurture her children and do household chores, whether she runs a multimillion-peso company or harvests rice in the fields. In return, her children are loyal to her and look on her as the greatest influence in their lives. She possesses a lot of power as the emotional center of the family. Yet she usually defers to her husband, the head of the household.

Most wealthy Filipinas either help in their husbands' businesses or pursue their own careers, some earning more than their husbands. Few educated women opt for the life of a housewife.

INTERNET LINKS

http://gabrielaphilippines.wordpress.com/
This is a blog about the organization Gabriela Philippines and its activities.

www.mongabay.com/reference/country_studies/philippines/SOCIETY.html
This site provides a comprehensive look at Filipino society.

LIFESTYLE

A young man pedaling side-car on a city street in Manila.

7

FILIPINOS, IT IS SAID, ARE MALAY IN family, Spanish in love, and American in ambition.

Three centuries of Spanish colonization and 50 years of U.S. rule have shaped a Filipino, or *Pinoy* (PEE-noi), lifestyle that combines Malay warmth, Latin charm, and American taste to produce a complex culture in which what you see may not always be what you get.

ATTITUDES

HIYA One of the keys to the Filipino character is the sense of *hiya* (HEE-ya), meaning "shame," which approximates the general Asian notion of "face" or reputation.

Hiya refers to Filipinos' concern for social conformity and suggests their deep immersion in communal tradition. It is also associated with self-esteem, something Filipinos prize above material comfort.

A Filipino's self-esteem depends on how society esteems him or her. A Filipino who is criticized in public loses social approval and consequently suffers *hiya*. This is why Filipinos react violently to public insults.

Conversely one avoids harming another's self-esteem by never openly telling them that they are being foolish or that they smell bad. If Filipinos value their own and their neighbors' "face," they must learn *pakikisama* (pa-KI-ki-SUM-ma), the art of maintaining smooth interpersonal relationships, to make life easier and succeed in society.

PAKIKISAMA This attitude prioritizes community over individual. Following the *pakikisama* guideline, a person tends to accept the majority decision rather than express disagreement with the opinion of the group.

Filipino time means that you will be at an occasion anywhere between 30 minutes and 1 hour late. To remedy this, people tend to set appointments an hour early, anticipating Filipino time.

Likewise, if a girl wants to turn down a date with her neighbor's son, rather than openly express her dislike for the boy, she will say that she has to study for an exam. This way, she avoids causing his family to lose face and helps keep relations between the two households friendly.

Filipinos dislike confrontation and are averse to breaking a congenial atmosphere with dissent. Criticism is made through a go-between or through light banter and teasing.

Pakikisama also includes a high sensitivity to social propriety, or *delicadeza* (DE-lee-ka-DE-za). Filipinos do not look favorably on guests who overstay their welcome, for example, or on people who take advantage of a position of power to enrich themselves.

To Filipinos sincerity does not necessarily mean directness. The Filipino concept of sincerity includes a genuine concern for the feelings of others.

For example, when asked for a favor, they may say "yes," even if they cannot grant it, so as not to embarrass the person making the request. When invited to a social function, they may not respond if they cannot attend. They may consider the invitation to be simply a polite gesture and not binding. They want to avoid being ungracious and offending the person inviting them. In short, Filipinos regard as sincere people who try to stay true to what society expects of them.

Pakikisama has made an excellent host out of the Filipino, who will give the best food and best room in the house to a visitor, welcome or otherwise. Ironically this hospitality was read as a sign of servility and inferiority by the early colonizers.

FILIPINO HUMOR

Filipinos have a great sense of humor, and they typically approach life in a lighthearted manner. Indeed they have such a strong *joie de vivre* that they seem to be laughing at something all the time. There are few things Filipinos take too seriously. They poke fun at the neighbor's curtains, the latest fashion trends and movie stars, a First Lady's predilection for kitsch, and even their empty wallets.

Pakikisama has no exact equivalent in English, but can be roughly defined as "getting along" or submitting to group will.

Imagine a Filipino guest dressed to the nines making a grand entrance to a party. Suddenly he slips and falls flat on his face. What does he do? He stands up, smiles, and challenges the other guests: "*O, kaya ba ninyo iyan*?" ("Can you do that?")

Humor can also be political, and the Filipino people have had a lot of practice poking fun at their politicians. More than the speeches of the opposition, it was the Marcos and Benigno jokes that appealed to the people in 1986. Exposing issues became a cinch through jokes and puns: "Marcos, *ano ang problema ng bayan? Kapitalismo, Pyudalismo, Imperialismo, Ikaw mismo!*" ("Marcos, what are the problems of the country? Capitalism, Feudalism, Imperialism, Yourself!")

Estrada was a more recent target for political humorists, especially on the Internet. At one website, a visitor posted this remark: "Marcos and [Estrada] are both men who have proven something. Marcos proved that you can be very rich if you become president. [Estrada] proved that we don't need a president."

COSMOPOLITAN MANILA

Words that describe Manila emphasize its contrasts . . . mélange, baroque, eclectic, collage, hodgepodge, potpourri.

Chinese spring rolls are dipped in vinegar and garlic, not soy sauce; 16th-century churches stand in the vicinity of skyscrapers; American pop music is used on the soundtracks of Philippine films; Chinatown karaoke joints play Spanish love songs.

On the road, a BMW stops beside a tricycle (the Philippine trishaw) at a red light, while street children peer into the car windows, begging. Politicians meet in a coffee shop to discuss the next election.

A typhoon arrives and school classes are suspended; movie houses make a killing. Even in the harshest of situations, Manileños know how to have a good time, constantly looking out for the best restaurant, the hottest dance club, and the trendiest fashion.

Two Filipino women laughing heartily.

Young men brave rush-hour traffic and pickpockets to catch a basketball game on television, where they can see their favorite player make a three-point basket.

THE COUNTRYSIDE

In the barrio, or village, people lead communal lives, sharing daily activities from washing clothes to planting rice. Backyards run together; fences are built only to separate houses from the roads. Villagers visit the local convenience store not just to buy things but also to exchange news.

Time goes by slowly, measured not by the hour but by the season: sowing or harvesting. Nevertheless modernity is creeping into even the most remote parts of the country.

Electrification projects bring light at the flick of a switch to more and more villages, while new telecommunication networks close gaps of distance, connecting villages to one another and to the cities and facilitating rural development.

The Philippines has the most expensive consumer prices for electricity in all of Asia.

Children in Ati village enjoying an afternoon together. There is a strong sense of community in the villages.

Because extending the power grid to rural areas is a costly procedure, the Philippines is advocating solar power to generate electricity in the rural areas.

KINSHIP TIES

Of all relationships, that of the family is the most basic, the strongest, and the most enduring. The family typically consists of the father, mother, and siblings, but can extend to distant relatives as well as close friends and loyal servants. The *compadrazgo* (COM-pud-DRAS-co) system brings non-blood relations into the family and enables the poor peasant to establish kinship ties with the richest people in the village.

The Filipino is usually not seen as an individual but as part of a family or community. Everyone belongs to a group, and the individual's identity is based on his or her kinship group. During social occasions, for instance, one tends to remain a stranger until one's kinship group is determined; interaction flows smoothly after mutual relatives, friends, classmates, colleagues, or townsfolk have been identified.

Personal independence is not of prime importance, and going it alone is simply seen as disliking one's family. Most adults who continue to live with their parents are not considered weak or childish, but devoted.

Strong kinship ties are the Filipino's best coping mechanism during critical times; they offer a strong support system that never fails to pull people through. However, these ties are also a social bane. Corporate and political nepotism can be rationalized as being helpful to one's family. Often Filipinos are torn between their official duties and their kinship obligations. This contradiction and duality are very much a part of Filipino identity and society.

BIRTH

Birth is usually an occasion everyone welcomes, as they speculate over the baby's gender and name and, later, which parent or uncle or aunty the baby takes after.

It is common for members of the same family to work for the same company. In fact, many collective bargaining agreements state that preferential hiring will be given to family members.

Boys at the back of a church in Mindanao.

In rural areas, most women give birth at home. The placenta is buried beneath the house, often with an object symbolizing what the parents hope the child will grow up to be. In the cities, this practice is prohibited by the health authorities.

The first religious ritual for a Filipino baby born into a Catholic family is baptism. For the occasion, the parents invite sponsors to be the godparents of the child. The role of the godparents is to guide and advise the child in coping in a harsh environment and to take over the upbringing of the child should the parents lose their ability to do so.

This system, called *compadrazgo*, is supposed to ensure the child's social and financial future. But in reality, it is a way of networking and showing off one's influential contacts.

THE GROWING-UP YEARS

Bringing up children is a communal affair in the Philippines. From the time children are born, they are handled with solicitude and tenderness by family members and friends. They are never left alone during the growing-up years, but are constantly surrounded by loved ones, if not siblings, then cousins. Filipino children are taught at an early age the value of good interpersonal relationships, and they practice it first within the family.

Filipino parents are generally unhurried and undemanding in training their children, but they are particular in nurturing concern for others and obedience. Children are essential in social gatherings, where they often sing and act for their elder relatives. Many Filipino children grow up to be good musicians, not least due to natural talent.

The onset of puberty is generally not a big occasion for celebration. Village boys prove their manhood by being circumcised without anesthesia, but boys in the cities are circumcised in a more clinical way.

DATING AND COURTSHIP

To avoid coming across as aggressive, a man has to be discreet when asking a woman out on a date. A friendly date, often in the company of friends, may be the starting point of a romantic relationship. The couple may then take the next step: going out on their own. The woman may bring a chaperone on solo dates.

Children are highly valued in Filipino communities.

A well-bred young lady in the city may show disinterest when a man woos her with flowers and chocolates and may even ignore him to test his sincerity.

In the countryside, a young man may serenade a young lady by singing beneath her window on a moonlit night.

When a couple decides they are ready, they will tell their family and friends about their romance, and then courtship begins.

It is said that courting a Filipina is to court her family as well. Traditionally a man first goes to the home of the woman he is interested in courting to introduce himself to her family, who will ask him many questions. After the first visit, he will bring gifts every time he comes again, in order to win approval from the woman's parents.

Modern courtships allow solo dates and candlelight dinners, but premarital sex is frowned on. Dating couples may go to dance clubs or rock concerts, but are expected to behave decently in public.

MARRIAGE

Filipinos choose their marriage partners, although they do seek family approval. The first step to the wedding is a formal proposal, called *pamanhikan* (PA-man-HEE-khan), which may be initiated by a go-between, a mutual relative or acquaintance of both families. A party is usually held, to which close relatives, sponsors, and a few friends are invited. The date and time of the wedding are set and church matters settled. Traditionally the groom's family pays for the wedding.

On the wedding day, the bride and groom stand at the altar with their sponsors. The priest prays over them and they exchange rings. Following Spanish tradition, the veil sponsors place a veil over the groom's shoulders and the bride's head, indicating the union of the two families. The cord sponsors then twist a silken or floral cord in the shape of the figure eight and loosely place each loop around the bride and groom's neck, symbolizing their lifelong bond. Finally the candle sponsors light candles on either side of the couple, a reminder of God's presence in the bond of marriage. Modern weddings include the Western tradition of the first kiss when the priest introduces them as newlyweds.

A reception follows, which in some areas includes a "money dance." Guests pin peso notes on the bride or groom in exchange for a dance, and the money the couple collects may be enough to start them out in life. The couple may also set free a pair of white doves during the reception to signify peace in their married life.

During the wake, the cleaned and embalmed body of the dead, placed in a coffin, is displayed at the house of the deceased or at a funeral home.

DEATH

Like birth, death is a family affair for Christian Filipinos. When there is a death, relatives and friends come to mourn with the bereaved, who welcome visitors with food and drink and tell them of the circumstances of the death. A wake is often a reunion of seldom-seen relatives and friends, who keep night vigils with the bereaved family. Immediate family members who live overseas return, lending joy to a sad occasion.

Although sending wreaths is customary, most people feel that giving money is more practical as it helps defray the cost of the funeral service. After the burial, overt grief is expected of the family. A husband or wife will cry or even faint at a spouse's burial.

The dead are always remembered in the Philippines. Nine days of prayers are held for the deceased after the burial, and death anniversaries are celebrated with a Mass or a visit to the grave.

INTERNET LINKS

http://myislandadventure.blogspot.com/2006/02/filipino-funeral. html

This site contains a Filipino-American girl's touching account of a Filipino funeral.

www.essortment.com/wedding-planning-filipino-wedding-traditions-53063.html

This is an interesting website on Filipino wedding traditions.

www.western-asian.com/filipinos/personality/75-the-art-of-filipino-togetherness-pakikisama-

This blog discusses what *pakikisama* means.

RELIGION

Mass at Baclaran Church in Luzon.

8

THE ANCIENT PEOPLE OF THE Philippines believed that the world was ruled by powerful spirits that manifested in nature.

They believed that these spirits could bring either happiness and good fortune or disease and death. They also believed that the god Bathala created heaven and earth and reigned supreme over the sea and river gods, the god of death, and other gods.

There are Filipinos who still worship rocks, trees, and animals, and perform rituals to ask the rain god for water or the earth god for a bountiful harvest. Although they can pray directly to the gods, they believe that their prayers will be heard more easily if they go through a priestess.

The Igorot place their dead in hanging coffins on limestone cliffs in Echo Valley, a sacred burial place.

The current president, Aquino, might face ex-communication from the Catholic Church for supporting the Reproductive Health Bill, the plan to distribute and give Filipino couples the choice to use contraceptives for artificial birth control. However, despite the possibility of ex-communication, Aquino said that he is not changing his position on contraception use.

There are also Filipinos who revere the spirits of their dead relatives, offering sacrifices to ask for guidance and protection.

For generations, one of the rites of passage for young boys of the Ifugao group in the northern region was carving from hardwood the image of the rice god, a central god in their culture.

Each family placed a pair of wooden rice god figures outside their home to watch over their granary. During ceremonial rituals, Ifugao elders poured the sacrificial blood of chickens over the images, praying for a good harvest.

Today Ifugao artisans practice their woodcarving tradition not so much to revere the rice god as to earn money from selling the images.

FOLK CHRISTIANITY

The Spanish missionaries arrived filled with a zealous desire to save the animist souls of the indigenous people. The missionaries built impressive churches and preached the virtuous path to salvation.

But the indigenous people found that medieval Castilian philosophy did not fit into their worldview, so they went on practicing animism behind the backs of the priests. The Spaniards may have imposed Christianity, but it would be inaccurate to say that the indigenous people fully accepted the foreign religion. Historians seem to see not the Christianizing of a people, but of their animistic practices. Christianity in the Philippines is really a unique folk variety, incorporating animistic beliefs.

One can easily recognize this in the practice of Christianity in the Philippines. For example, Filipinos have a strong devotion to the Virgin Mary and the Child Jesus. They acknowledge the Virgin Mary in many different capacities: as a shield against foreign invasion, as a protector during travel, and even as a fertility goddess. Filipino children often call her Mama Mary.

There are also cults devoted solely to the Child Jesus. Worshipers bathe images of the Santo Niño, or Holy Child. They clothe the statues in rich brocade, treating the Child Jesus as a princely guest in their homes. More than 50 icons of the Virgin Mary and the Child Jesus in the Philippines are said to be miraculous.

Another example of folk Christianity in the Philippines is the veneration of saints for prayers answered: for a good harvest, for rain, for the right spouse, for children.

Early Filipino converts may have seen features of their own rituals in Catholic sacraments. They may, for example, have associated the sacrament of baptism with their own healing rituals, which also used the symbolism of water.

The Spanish friar may have simply replaced the indigenous priestess as spiritual mediator. While the missionaries tried to completely destroy indigenous symbols and practices such as slavery and polygamy, some of the European Catholic practices they introduced blended with indigenous ritual practices. For example, they acted out biblical stories to teach the indigenous people about Christianity. Filipinos today act out the passion of Christ during Holy Week.

A faithful people, Filipinos look to religion for strength in times of trouble and attribute their accomplishments to divine guidance. What is important to them is that someone or something more powerful than themselves turns the wheel of life and may be counted on for help.

Catholic statues for sale. The majority of Filipinos are Catholic.

CATHOLIC PRACTICES

Like their fellow believers around the world, Catholics in the Philippines celebrate several sacraments that they believe are sources of spiritual life. Baptism is the first sacrament, celebrated soon after birth. First Holy Communion and Confirmation come when the child is older; they strengthen the believer's bond with God.

The sacrament of Holy Matrimony often marks the transition to responsible adulthood. The final sacrament, the Anointing of the Sick, is administered to people who are very ill and on the brink of death.

Holy Week is the last week of Lent and the week before Easter.

The elaborate altar of Saint Michael Archangel Church in Cebu.

Catholics pray as a community at Masses, novenas, and processions. In the family, they recite the rosary and say grace before meals. On Holy Thursday, worshipers visit churches; on Lenten Fridays, they abstain from eating meat; on Christmas Eve, they attend midnight Mass. When Catholics move to another house, they invite a priest to bless their new home before they settle in.

OTHER FAITHS

The Philippines, Asia's only Christian nation, is 80.9 percent Catholic and 7.3 percent Evangelical Christian.

Although Islam reached the Philippines before Christianity, it was contained by colonization. Filipino Muslims make up 5 percent of the population and live mostly in southern Mindanao.

The remaining 6.8 percent of the population profess other faiths. Taoism and Buddhism flourish in the countless Chinese communities. Hindus and Sikhs form a small minority and have their own religious enclaves.

CHURCHES

Almost every *barangay* has a church or chapel. In some parts of Manila and in most of the countryside, churches date back to the 16th or 17th century, products of the religious zeal of missionaries and the ingenuity and artistry of indigenous craftsmen. These churches were built solidly, to withstand typhoons and fires, but unfortunately did not always survive earthquakes. San Agustin, for example, has been severely damaged by several earthquakes.

A typical church has a squarish nave and a bell tower, and the priest's residence is located beside or behind the church. The bell tower was traditionally a measure of the church's prosperity—the taller it was, the wealthier its congregation. But more important, the bell serves to announce baptisms or weddings and to call the community to Mass.

Inside the church there is a central altar with a crucifix and shrines on the sides with the statues of saints.

FAITH HEALING

Faith healing—curing sickness without the aid of implements or drugs—was practiced in the Philippines especially before the advent of medical science. It was the domain of the *babaylan* (BA-BY-lun), or priestess, and later the herb doctor. Modernization did not eliminate faith healing. Filipinos who cannot afford to go to a hospital or clinic still turn to faith healers, who normally do not charge for their service for fear of losing their gift. Some faith healers claim to be guided by Catholic saints and may even have medical knowledge.

One form of faith healing is prayer—healers exorcise spirits of disease. Healers may also cure by touch, simply laying their hands on the sick person or using herbal concoctions and oils.

Most faith healers cure while in a trance. The most dramatic, most controversial form of faith healing is psychic surgery. The healer, using just

Muslims attending Friday prayers at the Golden Mosque in Quiapo.

A sacrament is a sacred rite recognized as having particular importance and significance.

the hands, opens up the body of the sick person and extracts a tumor or any diseased part. No anesthesia is used because apparently no pain is felt.

Reports of successful operations have raised intense debate. Medical doctors who remain unconvinced claim it is all a sham, that the psychic surgeon conceals in his hand a bloodied cotton ball and the extracted tissue is actually the liver of a chicken or pig.

Psychic surgery made U.S. tabloid headlines in March 1984 when entertainer Andy Kaufman, diagnosed with large cell carcinoma (a rare lung cancer), traveled to the Philippines for a six-week course of psychic surgery. Practitioner Jun Labo claimed to have removed large cancerous tumors and Kaufman declared that he believed this cancer had been removed. Kaufman died from renal failure as a consequence of a metastatic lung cancer on May 16, 1984.

On the other hand, there are the patients who testify to the power of psychic healing. Is it possible that spiritual power can open and close the body without pain or blood? Shaman or sham, the faith healer will remain "open for business" so long as people believe.

BELIEF IN MIRACLES

The mysticism surrounding many Catholic festivals in the Philippines reflects a strong belief in miracles. From a young age, Filipino children hear stories about apparitions of the Virgin Mary and religious icons that weep or bleed. Although for believers, these supernatural phenomena form the basis of "miracle faith," skeptics call it superstition.

In 1948 Teresita Castillo, a Carmelite novice in Lipa city in Batangas province, was reported to have seen an apparition of the Virgin Mary standing on a cloud, dressed in white, a golden rosary in her hand. According to Teresita, she received the vision 19 times and the apparition asked for penance and prayer to be offered for the clergy.

There were also accounts of hundreds of rose petals falling from the sky, each bearing a different holy image, such as the Virgin Mary holding a crucifix, the Last Supper, the Holy Family, and the crucified Jesus with three women at the foot of the cross. In 1991 there were reports of crosses of light appearing on frosted glass panels. Reports of crosses of light were first heard in 1988 in California and later in Seattle, Canada, and Washington, D.C., before showing up in the Philippines.

ANCIENT AMULETS

The *anting-anting* (UN-ting-UN-ting) are ancient amulets or talismans, passed down through a bloodline from one generation to the next. They may come in the form of a bracelet, necklace, or ring, and their owners may wear it like a medal. Each has a unique design, and many consist of spell-like inscriptions on pieces of cloth, bark, or paper.

No shaman alive today knows for sure how the first *anting-anting* came into existence. It is said that they were created in dark times when evil creatures roamed the islands. The *anting-anting* empowered the wearer to fight evil and protect the weak. In pre-Spanish times, every village had shamans, many known for their ability to make the *anting-anting*.

The *anting-anting* were said to give the wearer different powers—spiritual, physical, and psychic—and to protect them against bullets and poisonous snakes. There have been instances in the past when soldiers, thinking the *anting-anting* could make them invincible, rushed unarmed toward the enemies' guns, with fatal consequences.

It was also alleged that if a sick person possessed an amulet, he would not die until he bequeathed the amulet to a younger relative. There were supposedly even talismans that could make a person fall in love with the wearer. Owners of the *anting-anting* had to perform certain rituals at specific times to preserve the magical powers of the talismans.

Filipinos today use talismans or amulets mainly for good luck in their businesses and for protection from accidents and natural disasters. There are stalls in Quiapo, Manila, selling talismans, which the vendors claim have powers to help people in business, relationships, and sickness.

However, these modern-day lucky charms are not the same as the *anting-anting* of old that were supposed to give the wearer supernatural powers.

In Filipino films, the wearer of a magic amulet, the *agimat* (anting-anting) gains superhuman strength, invisibility, heightened senses, self-healing, and elemental powers. With it, the person can also shoot or fire lightning via their hands, or generate electricity throughout one's body. The person can also perform telekinesis, stop a live bullet, and basically be invincible.

FOLK BELIEFS

Early Filipinos believed in a soul and life after death. The indigenous groups have preserved this ancient belief. The Bagobo of southeastern Mindanao believe in the existence of two souls within each individual, one good and one evil. The Bukidnon believe that there are seven souls within a person, and these souls merge and migrate to Mount Balatocan after death. Most acknowledge the possibility of spirits coming back to earth; they have invented prayers and rituals to lead spirits to the afterlife.

Christianity reinforced belief in the afterlife, and indigenous rituals incorporated Christian elements, such as a cross or holy water used to subdue pagan creatures of the underworld.

Christianity has not been able to stem folk beliefs in fairies, elves, and other unseen beings. Filipinos often say *"Tabi tabi po"* (TA-bi TA-bi po) to excuse themselves for fear of stepping on elves. A pregnant woman is never left alone so that no hungry spirit, or *asuang* (AS-wahng), can eat her baby. If a child suddenly falls ill, the parents suspect that an earth spirit is the culprit.

Such beliefs and behaviors show that Filipinos recognize worlds other than their own and that they are willing to straddle the fence between logic and mystery.

MYTHS AND LEGENDS

People create myths in order to make sense of things and events in the world that cannot be otherwise explained. Based on their worldview and environment, early Filipinos tried to answer the question of where they came from by weaving creation legends.

One legend about the origin of the Filipinos goes like this: between heaven and earth blew a sea wind and a land wind. The winds married and brought forth a reed or bamboo. A bird pecked at the bamboo, breaking it in two, and from the bamboo emerged Silalak, the first man, and Sibabay, the first woman. They married and gave birth to the first Filipinos.

A version of the legend says that Silalak and Sibabay were siblings, forced to mate in order to propagate the human race. Another version says the woman and the man emerged from separate bamboos and had no knowledge of each other before they met, married, and bore children.

The belief that the bird is the creature that unlocked human life suggests an ancient reverence for birds. The Tagalog identify their chief god, Bathala, in a blue bird.

A northern Luzon legend explains that the sky used to be low, but a maiden pounded her rice so vigorously that her wooden pole pushed the sky high. On the clouds she hung her jewelry, and they twinkled as stars.

Legends also help shape ideals, as in the legend of Maria ng Makiling, the beautiful goddess who inspired José Rizal with the purity of her love, even for a lesser mortal. Maria had the power to either unite people in love or separate them if they were unworthy of each other. She fell in love with a mortal man who was in love with a mortal woman. Maria was heartbroken, but she gave the couple her blessings anyway, and she never revealed her beautiful self to mortal eyes again.

INTERNET LINKS

http://folktales.webmanila.com/
This is a collection of fascinating Filipino folktales, myths, and legends.

www.aidan.co.uk/photos20-Churches%20of%20the%20Philippines.php
This site contains beautiful photos of churches in Manila.

www.librarylink.org.ph/featarticle.asp?articleid=114
This website provides a comprehensive description of the various types of *anting-anting* with lovely pictures.

Santelmo, or Santo Elmo, is a fireball seen by dozens of Filipinos, especially those living in the Sierra Madre Mountains. It was scientifically explained as electric fields that have diverged from the lines. However, the sightings were reported since the Spanish era (16th–19th centuries). There were also sightings in the Alps and the Himalayas.

LANGUAGE

A newspaper vendor selling newspapers. While the national language is Filipino, English is an official language and the majority of Filipinos are able to read and speak English.

9

MORE THAN 100 LANGUAGES ARE spoken in the Philippines. The eight major ones are Tagalog, Cebuano, Ilocano, Bicolano, Kapampangan, Pangasinan, Hiligaynon, and Samarnon.

Tagalog is also spoken by Filipinos living in the United States, Canada, the United Kingdom, Saudi Arabia, and elsewhere. Philippine languages belong to the Malayo-Polynesian family; each has dialects specific to towns or barrios in the city or municipality where the language is concentrated.

English is an official language in the Philippines, but the national language is Filipino, which is based on Tagalog and other languages.

In the Philippines, there are between 120 and 175 languages, depending on the method of classification.

English is the language of instruction in most schools.

Even though Filipinos speak different dialects, English has served as the linking language throughout the different regions and is taught throughout all the schools in the Philippines.

Filipino is spoken in the Metro Manila area and in the southern Luzon Tagalog provinces. It is understood by 90 percent of the population and is the language of instruction in many schools. The government intends to make Filipino the language of administration nationwide.

FOREIGN LANGUAGES

It is no surprise that English is the most widely used foreign language in the Philippines; it has been the language of instruction in schools throughout the country for almost eight decades. It is still the language of instruction in universities and the medium of government and mass communication. English serves as a link language among Filipinos who speak different regional languages and is spoken throughout the country, especially during business negotiations.

The Philippines is the third-largest English-speaking nation in the world, following the United States and India. Filipinos speak a variety of English culled mainly from the United States and infused with the idiosyncrasies

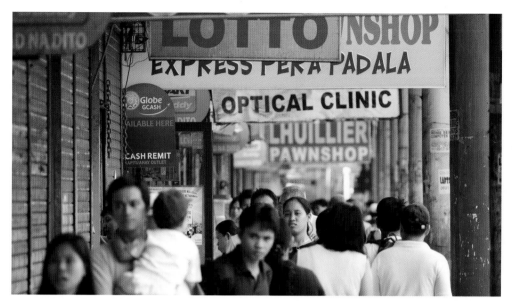

Philippine languages have been influenced over the years by other cultures such as the Chinese and Indians.

of local languages and dialects. In informal situations, Filipinos often use a combination of languages, creating a hybrid called Taglish (Tagalog-English).

Before 1987 Spanish was a required subject in school. Spanish speakers are now rare in the Philippines, although most Filipinos have a working knowledge of the language. The national language is liberally laced with Spanish words.

Hokkien or Fujianese is mostly spoken by the Chinese and has contributed significantly to the vocabulary of Philippine languages. Indian influences can be seen in ancient scripts as well.

A MIXED BAG OF NAMES

Many Filipinos bear Iberian-sounding surnames without having Iberian ancestry. This is because of a 19th-century Spanish decree that required all Filipinos to use a Spanish surname.

In fact, in many Philippine towns, the people bear last names starting with the same letter of the alphabet. The Spaniards allocated surnames by

Many children are named after the saint whose feast day falls on the child's birthday.

town, reserving surnames starting with the letter "A" for people in the capital. The outlying towns received surnames starting with subsequent letters: "B" in the second town, "C" in the third, and so on. This made it easy to identify a person and trace his or her municipal origins.

The choice of first names was dictated by a person's birthdate. A Filipino couple was likely to name their baby after the saint whose feast day fell on the child's birthday.

Some women have the name Maria, abbreviated as Ma., before their name, as a sign of respect for the Virgin Mary.

BODY TALK

TOUCHING Filipinos are a "touchy" people in that relatives and close friends make a lot of physical contact in greeting and in conversation. A young Filipino greets an older person with a gesture of respect called *mano* (MAHN-no), or "hand." The young person puts the back of the older person's hand on his or her forehead.

Relatives and friends generally do a cheek-to-cheek greeting called *beso-beso* (BAE-so BAE-so), or "kiss-kiss." However, people of the opposite sex prefer to shake hands when meeting for the first time, especially at business meetings and social occasions, and the man is expected to wait for the woman to extend her hand.

EYEBROW HELLO Filipinos may say hello without words, but with an upward nod of the head and a quick lift of the eyebrows. If the eyebrow "flash" lingers too long, it signifies a query.

GESTURES OF HOSTILITY Staring suggests provocation and may endanger the curious. Standing with arms akimbo signifies arrogance, except in a teacher who is reprimanding a student or a policeman confiscating a driver's license.

GESTURES OF RESPECT Filipinos may greet their superiors with a nod. When walking between two people in conversation, one says, "Excuse me" and bows, extending the hand in front. To get someone's attention, one does not shout or point a finger. Filipinos make eye contact and signal with a nod or with the hand, palm facing down.

SMILE Filipinos do everything with a smile—they praise with a smile, criticize with a smile, condole with a smile, take life's trials with a smile. A confrontation is best avoided, but if it is necessary, a smile is the best way to start. An embarrassing moment is covered with a smile, while allegations are dismissed with a knowing grin.

INTERNET LINKS

www.ethnologue.com/show_country.asp?name=PH
This site includes a comprehensive listing of every known language in Philippines.

www.worldbusinessculture.com/Filipino-Business-Communication-Style.html
This website provides a guide to communicating successfully in Philippines.

Smiling is considered the right reaction to situations beyond one's control, a Philippine reality. Historically Filipinos have had little control over the environment. Typhoons, crop failure, invaders, and other such disasters and disturbances were taken in their stride and even expected.

ARTS

10

ANCIENT PHILIPPINE LITERATURE consisted of myths, legends, songs, riddles, proverbs, epics, and tales that touched daily life.

Folk songs depicted the lifestyles of the indigenous groups and their hopes and aspirations. Some invented work songs, such as the rowing song of the Tagalog and the rice-pounding song of the Kalinga. The Ilocano composed war songs, love songs, and death chants. The Cebuano and Bontoc sang dirges and lamentations, recalling the deeds of the deceased.

Epics and tales explained the creation of the world, the landscape, and animals. The epics of the Maranao and Ifugao often revolved around supernatural events.

When the Spaniards colonized the archipelago, they brought religion-based morality and passion plays and stories based on the lives of the saints. By the 18th and 19th centuries, however, a group of educated Filipinos had emerged. They began writing novels, poems, and other forms of literature in Spanish, as well as in the vernacular. Intellectuals who studied in Europe penned anti-Spanish, anti-clergy texts, not with a Filipino audience in mind, but a Spanish one.

Francisco Baltazar, known by his pen name, Balagtas, wrote allegorical poetry to depict the injustices of the Spaniards in the Philippines. Balagtas's most famous piece was *Florante at Laura*. The greatest works of the period, and perhaps in all of Philippine literary history, were the novels of José Rizal. Rizal's best-known works were *Noli Me Tangere* and *El Filibusterismo*, both depicting the abuses of the Spaniards and the nationalistic aspirations of the Filipinos.

Doctrina Christiana, written by Fray Juan de Plasencia, was the first book printed in the Philippines.

97

A book restorer working on restoring the original handwritten novels by national hero, José Rizal.

LITERATURE IN ENGLISH AND FILIPINO

Barely 20 years after American missionaries set up the first English class in the islands, Filipinos began writing stories in this foreign language.

The 1950s and early 1960s are considered the golden age of Philippine literature in English, with writers such as Francisco Arcellana, Bienvenido Santos, and the most famous, Nick Joaquín.

With the surge of nationalism in the 1960s and 1970s, many writers shifted to Filipino as a medium, and the regional languages were given due importance. Social realism became the main literary style.

Filipinos today are big fans of popular culture. While many may like Shakespeare, they also love comics. *Sari-sari* stores (convenience stores) often rent comic books so that patrons can follow their favorite series.

DANCE

Tinikling has been named the Filipino national dance.

Philippine dance reflects Malay and Spanish influences. The *singkil* (SING-kil) performed by a graceful Filipina between bamboo poles never fails to entertain audiences. The *jota* (HO-ta) and *curacha* (coo-RA-cha) of Spain are the highlight of school programs and fiestas. Indigenous dances imitate nature; for instance, the movement of birds. The famous bamboo dance, the *tinikling* (ti-NI-kling), mimics the agile movements of a bird as it traipses along reeds. There are also dances to celebrate a courtship or a warrior's victory or to mourn death.

Filipinos love to dance, whether at a village festival, at a club on a Saturday night, or in the living room at home. Hardly anywhere else in the world can television viewers watch so many dance performances and contests as in the Philippines. The Cultural Center of the Philippines in Manila is the national hub for ballet performances.

Filipino dancers performing the traditional *tinikling* dance.

MUSIC

Music is a part of everyday life in the Philippines. Filipinos sing in the bathroom, in the kitchen, and even in the office. They hum a melody when stuck in traffic. Children learn to play the guitar, piano, violin, or other musical instruments from an early age, and the more gifted go on to participate in international music festivals and competitions.

Contemporary Philippine music may be Western in sound, yet it remains Filipino in character—in its sentimentality, romantic content, and mellow mood. Although many songs originally written in English have been translated into Philippine languages, listeners are increasingly choosing to listen to original local compositions, especially those in the Filipino language.

Clubs in the Philippines play folk, jazz, rock-and-roll, and other kinds of music. Concerts and live acts are frequent. The Philippine Philharmonic Orchestra performs at the Cultural Center in Manila and in other big cities around the country. Filipinos in Manila can enjoy free open-air concerts at Rizal Park on Sundays and Paco Park on Fridays.

Filipino hip-hop is one of the hottest genres in the Philippines today.

Filipino musicians also perform in other parts of Asia and elsewhere on the international circuit. Regine Velásquez was voted "Favorite Artist for the Philippines" at the 2002 MTV Asia Awards, where she sang a duet with American pop star Mandy Moore.

Another Filipina who has made it big with her singing (and acting) talent is Lea Salonga, who at the tender age of 17 landed the lead role in the musical *Miss Saigon,* for which she won a Tony for Best Actress.

A man surrounded by guitars and a harp in a store on Mactan Island.

Salonga was also in the Broadway show of *Les Misérables*, as Eponine.

Ethnic music lives on in the indigenous communities. Traditional instruments include a harp called the *kubing* (KHU-bing), a gong called the *kulintangan* (KHU-lin-THA-ngan), and a bamboo nose flute. The International Bamboo Organ festival held in the Philippines every year attracts participants from other parts of the world as well. Although there are Filipinos who want to preserve ethnic music in its pure state, there are also those who wish to incorporate it into contemporary music.

DRAMA AND THEATER

Early Philippine drama was performed as part of rituals observed at major stages of life such as birth and death as well as in work activities such as planting and harvesting. Like early literature, early drama was enmeshed in everyday life, without stage, lights, or camera.

European drama came with the Christian evangelists. The *cenáculo* (si-NAH-KU-loh) emerged as a distinctly Philippine version of the passion play. The musical operetta called the *zarzuela* (sahr-SWHE-lah) has today evolved into other forms of contemporary theater.

Dramas in English were first performed in the universities on topics such as historical events and domestic problems. In the late 1960s, with the resurgence of nationalism, writers began using Filipino, and drama was seen as the most potent art form for exposing national issues.

Present-day theater in Filipino has reached high standards, even as plays in English continue to be written and performed by university student groups and professional theater troupes.

PAINTING AND FILM

Painting in the early Spanish years was reserved for religious purposes. Secular paintings increased in the 19th century, serving as souvenirs for foreign visitors. These paintings showed the indigenous people in their traditional dress. Damián Domingo y Gabor (1790—1832) was the best-known painter in this genre. He set up the country's first fine-arts school. In 1884 Juan Novicio Luna and Felix Resurrección Hidalgo won awards in Spain and Paris for their paintings.

The Philippines' domestic film industry is still struggling to gain acceptance and a footing amid international competition.

More recent noted painters include César Legaspi (1917—94) and Vicente Manansala (1910—81).

Filipino films face intense competition at the local box office. The 21st century heralded the start of the dramatic decline of the Filipino movie industry. Filipino viewers throng the theaters to watch Hollywood films, but the response to homegrown films is lukewarm. In 2001 then president Gloria Macapagal Arroyo asked town and city mayors to reduce the entertainment tax on movies, but only a few obliged. Nevertheless local film companies are working to improve the quality of their products in various genres such as drama, comedy, action, and horror. There are directors who focus on creating films that not only tackle the realities of Philippine life, but also bring out the best in Philippine cinematic artistry.

Films that address serious social issues can often provoke controversy. In 2001 *Live Show*, a documentary film directed by José Javier Reyes, was banned by the government for its "pornographic" portrayal of sex workers. More than 300 filmmakers, actors, and students in Manila protested the ban. Screened at film festivals in the United States, Europe, and Australia, *Live Show* earned acclaim for depicting the poverty that forces Filipino men and women into the sex industry.

TRADITIONAL CRAFTS

Many indigenous communities have their own handweaving traditions, using different natural materials to produce textiles with a variety of colors and designs.

The T'boli weave dyed tree bark strands into geometric designs. Yakan weaves are a spectrum of color. Filipinos from the Panay islands and Mindanao use silk or the fibers of the pineapple and abaca. Weavers in Ilocos Sur create checked and striped patterns, while those in Abra base their designs on the images of their gods.

Although many weavers as part of a tradition passed on their craft from generation to generation, for some the craft is simply a source of income to

A T'boli tribeswoman using a traditional loom to weave.

support their families. They can earn money from the sale of their products to tourists.

However, there is a real concern that the art of handweaving is becoming extinct. The younger generations do not have an interest in learning their parents' craft. Local governments are thus seeking to revive traditional weaving by encouraging handweaving in schools. Other ways used to promote the art include displaying handwoven cloth in trade shows and using it to design fashionable clothing.

Woodcarving and furniture-making have produced the most intricate crafts from trees. For Paete in Laguna, woodcarving is a town industry, while the town of Betis in Pampanga has the highest reputation for wooden furniture.

Basketry is a very developed craft among indigenous communities in the Mountain province, Mindanao, and Palawan.

Traditionally woven baskets are used by their makers to catch fish or store grain or other goods; yet these baskets adorn the houses of the wealthy because of the skill and artistry they exhibit. A Philippine basket may be made from one material or a combination such as bamboo and rattan, depending on the province or town its maker comes from.

Other crafts for which the Philippines is famous are the shellcraft of Cebu and the silver filigree of Baguio.

The Community Crafts Association of the Philippines (CCAP) is a nonprofit organization in Quezon city that serves more than 2,000 artisans from all over the archipelago. Founded in 1973, the CCAP aims to improve the social conditions of Filipinos living in villages and slums by providing them with assistance in marketing their traditional crafts.

INTERNET LINKS

www.philital.com/english/tourism/tourism_craftsb.htm
This site contains a comprehensive listing of every type of Filipino craftwork you can imagine.

The Philippines, being one of Asia's earliest film industries, remains undisputed in terms of the highest level of theater admission in Southeast Asia. Over the years, however, the film industry has registered a steady decline in movie viewership, from 131 million in 1996 to 63 million in 2004. The film industry is rife with problems: domination by Hollywood movies, rampant piracy, overtaxation, and a poor economy.

LEISURE

A boy paddling an outrigger on the clear waters off Malapascua Island in Cebu.

11

F ILIPINO CHILDREN HAVE few toys but many playmates. For many children in the Philippines, toys are a luxury. Because they are usually surrounded by relatives and friends, their play activities tend to involve a lot of games and social interaction.

They go to the backyard or the street and indulge in an hour of *luksong-tinik* (look-SONG-tee-nik), in which a player jumps over a stick or over the outstretched arms of playmates; *sungka* (song-KAH), in which players collect shells or stones in their "home" hole in a specially made wooden board; *siklot* (SEEK-loot), which is similar to jacks; *sipa*

Men playing a game of pool in the streets.

The Philippines Basketball Association (PBA) is the first and oldest professional basketball league in Asia and the second oldest in the world after the National Basketball Association (NBA) in the United States.

Cockfighting is a centuries-old bloodsport, popular since the times of ancient Persia, Greece, and Rome. It is still practiced in Asia and South America. In the Philippines cockfighting is virtually a religion, and matches are a weekly "duty." Well-heeled businessmen and dirt-poor peasants fill the galleries of cockpits on Sunday afternoons, playing a game of chance with plumed warriors. Cockfight aficionados will beg or borrow to bet on their favorite birds. Owners groom their prized possessions, massaging and exercising the birds.

Finger-play precedes the actual match. A kristo (KRIS-toh) stands in the center of the pit, taking bets. Without paper or calculator, he is somehow able to accurately match bets with faces. He moves around with arms outstretched and fingers extended, signaling to the gamblers which bird is receiving bets at any particular moment. The gamblers point any number of fingers up, down, or sideways to signal their bets.

Then the match begins. The trained birds, equipped with sharp spurs, or gaffs, claw at each other in a battle to the death. The contest ends when one bird runs away or dies. The winning bird must seal his victory by pecking at the loser twice. This ancient sport has come under heavy criticism as extreme animal cruelty.

(SEE-pah), in which players kick a palm or paper ball; as well as hide-and-seek, blind man's buff, and kite flying.

Adults play chess, bingo, or mahjong, a game of Chinese origin.

No fiesta is complete without special games such as cracking-the-pot, in which blindfolded players try to hit a hanging pot using a pole (like a game of piñata); trying to hook a ring while riding a bicycle; stepping on one another's shoulders to reach reward money at the top of a greased bamboo pole; and sack racing.

Animal competitions are also popular. Carabao races and horse fights are held in some parts of the country, but the most popular animal sport is cockfighting.

Off-road enthusiasts navigating the undulating terrain at the La Paz Sand Dunes National Geographical Monument.

SPORTS

Sports and recreational activities in the Philippines vary according to the terrain. Filipinos engage in outdoor sports such as tennis, jogging, baseball, volleyball, track and field events, soccer, and golf. Bowling, boxing, and weightlifting are popular indoor alternatives. Game fishing is also a very popular activity.

The highlands beckon to mountain climbers and hang-gliders, while the coasts draw swimmers, scuba divers, and windsurfers. Just about any beach in the Philippines offers great snorkeling sites, some coral within 82 feet (25 m) of the shore. But the islands' grand passion is basketball, with the Philippine Basketball Association (PBA) driving the sport's popularity for more than 25 years.

FUN IN THE TOWNS AND VILLAGES

Entertainment and recreation in the countryside coincide with the seasons. During the hot summer months, young people look forward to picnics. When the rains come, they amuse themselves with the radio.

The Philippines has hosted several "World Slasher Cup" derbies, held twice a year and staged in Araneta Coliseum. The world's leading game fowl breeders gather twice a year during this event.

BASKETBALL

Basketball is the national obsession in the Philippines. If there is anything aside from politics that Filipinos from different generations—or even different genders—can fight about, it is basketball.

The basketball court is as common as the jeepney; no town plaza or college campus is without a court. Children create single-basket courts in street corners, or a flower pot in the backyard will do just fine. Although height does matter on the court, the lack of it does not seem to stop the smaller-built from venturing into the sport, by making up for their height disadvantage with speed.

Televised championship games attract millions of viewers, who watch with anticipation as their favorite teams battle for supremacy. To fans PBA teams are the object of admiration and loyalty. On a championship night everything comes to a standstill as energies focus on the game. After an exhausting finish, fans of the winning team celebrate, while those of the defeated team sigh in dismay, foreseeing the ribbing to come the next day.

With names such as Coca-Cola Tigers and FedEx Express, teams in the PBA are attractive product movers, and businesses pour huge amounts of advertising money into the games.

As soon as they are able, children go out into the streets to play. In most barrios, roads are an extension of the house. On moonlit nights, children play hide-and-seek and other local games.

Religious holidays are other occasions that provide a break from work in the fields. The most anticipated event is the patron saint feast day, the reason for the town fiesta.

When the fiesta is imminent, the carnival comes to town. Complete with rides, dice games, shooting, and ring booths, the carnival entertains the townspeople for a month or so, building up festive tension until the feast day arrives.

There is no tradition more Philippine than a fiesta. The town fiesta is a celebration of the pact between the people and their patron saint, an offer of thanksgiving to the saint for his or her protection over the community. The fiesta is also a time of baptisms, weddings, and family reunions.

During the fiesta, homes are open to everyone, including strangers, and the occasion shows Filipinos at their most hospitable. Carnivals, games, and beauty contests give the residents a chance to release the pent-up energy and stress from a year of toil.

A fiesta needs preparation. People spruce up their homes, cook special food, and pray for nine days. Preparations reach fever pitch as the feast day draws near, the air electric with anticipation.

On the day itself, people wear their Sunday best. Visitors are advised to eat only a small amount of food in the first house they visit because that is certainly not going to be the last. Wine and goodwill flow freely.

The carabao fiesta is celebrated in farming towns on the feast day of San Isidro in May. Farmers parade their groomed and decorated carabao around town. Then comes the carabao race, after which the beasts are guided to kneel as the priest blesses them. The seaside town of Pandan in Antique celebrates its fiesta in April in honor of Saint Vincent Ferrer. Pandan holds an annual boat-rowing competition during the fiesta.

The celebration climaxes with brass bands roaming the streets from dawn to dusk, sumptuous family meals at home, and the Mass and procession.

FUN IN THE CITY

The cities offer cosmopolitan pleasures such as shopping in mega malls, dining in luxurious restaurants, and enjoying movies in cinema complexes. Karaoke lounges dare anyone gutsy enough to take the microphone, while dance clubs are great places for Filipinos to indulge in their passion for

Women enjoying an afternoon of karaoke at a roadside stall in Mindanao.

dancing. Philippine television broadcasts a host of variety shows and soap operas for the housebound.

Museums offer a leisurely form of education. The National Museum in Manila and the Ayala Museum in Makati give visitors a good introduction to Philippine history and culture.

PLACES TO GO

For newcomers, the Philippines offers interesting historical sites that provide a crash course on local history and culture. In Manila there is Fort Santiago, a mute testament to colonial oppression; Casa Manila, a replica of the Spanish stone house, or *bahay na bato* (bah-AY na ba-TO); the Monument at Rizal Park; and relics of contemporary history such as the Malacañang Palace museum, where one can enter Imelda Marcos's boudoir.

Outside Manila, there is the Rizal family house in Laguna, the Barosoain church in Bulacan, the Aguinaldo house in Cavite, the Magellan shrine in Cebu, and MacArthur's landing spot in Leyte.

If one wants a bird's-eye view of the different regional cultures, one goes to Nayong Pilipino, which contains replicas of important Philippine historical and scenic spots. Paco Park, one of the most pleasant nature spots in Manila, is the site of evening cultural-musical presentations featuring local and international talents.

NATURE TRIPS

Nature has blessed the Philippines with abundance as well as beauty. The weary soul can take refuge in any of the beautiful beaches around the country. Boracay, in the Visayas, is famous for stretches of white sand and a relatively isolated location.

Batangas, Mindoro, and Pangasinan are great for those who have just a few days to spare. El Nido, in Palawan, is famous for its underwater treasures. Pagsanjan, in Laguna, is noted for waterfalls and boatmen who deftly negotiate dangerous rapids.

Volcanic springs are popular tourist spots. Baguio is a favorite refuge during the hot summer months, the air cool and invigorating. Banaue, a mountain village farther north, presents a life as simple as it was centuries ago and a glorious morning view of the famous rice terraces.

INTERNET LINKS

http://digitista.blogspot.com/2011/05/wowed-by-carabaos-pulilan-carabao.html

This site provides a firsthand view of an overseas Filipina's experience of the carabao festival, with lovely pictures.

www.seasite.niu.edu./Tagalog/Filipino_Games/mga_larong_pilipino.htm

This website includes comprehensive descriptions of the traditional games that Filipino children play.

Most of the larger cities throughout the Philippines are home to some high-class casinos, often as part of one of the more upmarket hotels.

FESTIVALS

A young boy and girl smile widely at the annual
Sinulog Parade.

12

T HERE ARE FIVE RELIGIOUS events celebrated nationwide in the Philippines: Holy Thursday, Good Friday, and Easter in March/April; All Saints' Day on November 1; and Christmas on December 25.

LENT

Lent, the biggest religious season in the country, commemorates the death and resurrection of Jesus Christ. Although the season culminates in the joyous celebration of new life at Easter, the mood throughout Lent is somber in reflective anticipation of Christ's death and crucifixion. A blaze of color and dramatic festivals, however, lighten the atmosphere. The season of Lent begins with Ash Wednesday when priests draw a cross of ash on the foreheads of Catholic worshipers.

HOLY WEEK

The climax of Lent is Holy Week, which commemorates the week of Christ's death and resurrection. Palm Sunday ushers in Holy Week. In memory of Christ's entry into Jerusalem, people bring palm fronds to the church service to be blessed by the priest.

The folk aspect of Philippine Christianity is seen in a ritual called *pabasa* (pa-BA-sa), when the teachings of Christ are chanted. Flagellants beat their bare backs with glass-spiked leather thongs, not as an act of masochism, but in fulfillment of a *panata* (pa-NA-ta), or vow. The

The fiesta is part and parcel of Filipino life. Through good times and bad times, the fiesta must go on. Each city and barrio has at least one local festival of its own, usually on the feast of its patron saint, so that there is always a fiesta going on somewhere in the country.

devotee lives up to a promise to undergo the pain and humiliation of this penitential act in exchange for a granted request or a forgiven wrong. Some *pabasa* participants even go to the extent of having themselves tied or nailed to a cross on Good Friday.

An air of gloom descends on Good Friday. At mid-afternoon the last words of Christ are spoken and explained in the pulpits. In the evening a replica of Christ's bier is taken around the town in a procession.

At dawn on Easter, the meeting of the risen Christ and the Virgin Mary is reenacted. Two carriages, one carrying a figure of the risen Christ and the other a figure of the grieving Mary, are taken to opposite parts of town. They are to meet at a selected church, where children dressed as angels sing as they lift the mourning veil from the statue of the Virgin Mary. The two carriages are then brought into the church amid the joyous ringing of bells.

CHRISTMAS

Christmas in the Philippines begins as early as late October. Carols play over the radio, and classrooms, offices, and homes put on festive cheer with tinsel and ribbons, Christmas trees and lights.

The Holy Week procession of San Guillermo Church.

At home a replica of the Nativity scene, complete with shepherds and kings, is set up. By the window hangs a lantern, either in a riot of color or in the shape of a star.

Nine dawn Masses precede Christmas Day; rice cakes eaten after each Mass make rising early a little less difficult. On Christmas Eve the family gathers to eat a sumptuous meal after midnight Mass. On Christmas morning the children wake up to gifts from Santa Claus.

In a Bulacan town, Mary and Joseph's search for a place to stay just before the birth of their son is reenacted. The actors are turned away at every house they visit, finally finding shelter in a church.

Houses decorated for the annual Harvest Festival in Lucban. The festival honors the patron saint of farmers, San Isidro Labrador.

HONORING SAINTS

Almost all *barangays* and towns hold fiestas, but some fiestas are more famous than others.

In Manila the best-known fiesta is the feast of the Nazarene, patron saint of the capital's oldest—and central—district, Quiapo. In January thousands of devotees clog the main roads of Quiapo in a body-to-body procession. Leading the procession are male devotees called *hijo* (EE-ho), or sons, who pull a carriage bearing a figure of *Nuestro Padre Señor Jesús Nazareno* (Our Father, Jesus of Nazareth).

The figure of the Nazarene has allegedly been blackened by the constant libation of indigenous perfumes. Devotees have to push their way through a crowd in order to reach the figure and wipe a cloth or handkerchief on the face or hands of the icon; the devotees then use the "blessed" cloth or handkerchief to wipe themselves, following an ancient folk ritual.

Outside Manila, the most colorful fiesta is celebrated in May in Lucban, Quezon. This is the feast day of San Isidro de Labrador, the patron saint of farmers. Called the *pahiyas* (pa-hee-yahs), this fiesta is a thanksgiving for a good harvest, which is reflected in the food-based decorations that color the town during this fiesta.

The townspeople make thin, leaf-shaped wafers from pounded rice dyed pink, yellow, and other bright colors. These wafers, or *kiping* (kee-ping), are then used to make lanterns, flowers, and other hanging pieces to adorn windows, doors, and walls together with fruit, grains, and vegetables.

Towns situated near rivers celebrate their feast days with water parades. Icons mounted on water carriages are paraded along rivers rather than along streets. Devotees ride decorated *banca* (bun-ka) or immerse themselves in the river. Some riverside towns celebrate with water throwing, reminiscent of the world-famous Songkran water festival in Thailand.

Filipinos in Calumpit in Bulacan province throw water on one another on the feast day of John the Baptist, Calumpit's patron saint. There is also a water parade that features pagodas and brass bands. Manila, the Camiguin Islands, and various cities across the country also celebrate the feast of John the Baptist with water parades, processions, and boat races.

The village of Aliaga in Nueva Ecija celebrates the feast of John the Baptist with even more folk tradition. During the Taong Putik (Mud People) Festival, devotees visit people's homes, dressed in dry banana or coconut leaves and smeared with mud. At each home, they are given candles or gifts to be offered to the saint. The "mud people" then gather at the village church and give thanks to the saint for blessings received. An outdoor Mass follows, after which devotees carry an icon of the saint out of the church and into the streets.

FOLK FESTIVALS

Many folk festivals retain strong elements of animist religions, while incorporating Christian figures.

The Ati-Atihan of Kalibo in Aklan province is a local Mardi Gras held in honor of the Santo Niño. Revelers, their faces blackened with soot, go around town to the beat of drums and rhythmic shouts of "*Hala bira!*" The procession

The Santo Niño parade is part of the Ati-Atihan Festival in Kalibo.

snakes along the narrow streets of Kalibo. Women holding Santo Niño icons rub elbows with hedonists drunk on the heart-pounding beat of the mountain peoples.

May is the month of the Virgin Mary. Flores de Mayo, a flower festival in honor of the Virgin Mary, lasts through May. During this time, girls in the rural areas offer flowers in churches. Dressed in all their finery, the girls walk under flower arches amid candles and lights.

In the cities, however, the Flores de Mayo has virtually become a fashion show, and the designer gowns worn by the girls attract more attention than the devotions.

The month of flower offerings culminates with the Santacruzan, a one-day celebration in which the empress Helena's search for the Holy Cross is reenacted. The Santacruzan is a parade of biblical characters and allegorical figures.

January 1	*New Year's Day*
April 9	*Bataan Day*
May 1	*Labor Day*
June 12	*Independence Day*
December 30	*Rizal Day*

January 1, a nonreligious holiday, is always considered part of Christmas. The New Year is greeted with firecrackers and fireworks exactly at midnight, after which a lavish meal is shared. April 9 commemorates the bleakest time in Philippine history, when the combined American-Filipino forces were forced to surrender to the Japanese after a valiant last stand. June 12, 1898, was the first time the Filipinos declared their independence from a colonizer, the Spanish. This was made possible by the death of a great man, José Rizal, the most prominent advocate for reform in the Philippines during the Spanish colonial era, on December 30, 1896.

The traditional procession features the empress with her son, Constantine the Great, as well as biblical characters. Adorned icons of the Virgin Mary are paraded through streets lined with bamboo poles from which hang bundles of coins and bread, candies, and fruit.

Bacoor in Cavite province, where fishing is a major occupation, holds a fisherman's festival in May that features a boat procession. People praying for miracles and blessings wave leafy branches in the path of the pagoda-like boats to the sounds of a brass band and splashing water.

Bocaue, a town in Bulacan province, holds a river procession—the Pagoda-sa-Wawa festival—in July to commemorate the finding of a crucifix in the Bocaue River by an ancestor. A large replica of the historic Holy Cross of Wawa is paraded on a barge, followed by a fleet of fishing boats.

The Kadayawan is a five-day celebration originating among Davao's indigenous groups such as the Bagobo, Maranaw, and Mandaya. The festival is held in August in thanksgiving for a plentiful harvest.

The Kadayawan has become an extravagant event, with street dancing, a parade of floral floats, concerts, contests, exhibits of indigenous arts and customs, and fireworks displays. For Davaoeños the festival's significance runs deep, a celebration of their ethnic roots in thanking God for blessings received.

OTHER FESTIVALS

Chinese Filipinos set off their firecrackers to celebrate the Lunar New Year, the traditional Spring Festival. In the Philippines, a land with no spring, the Chinese give their friends *tikoy* (tee-coy), or glutinous rice cake; prepare red packets of money for children of friends and relatives; and invite lion dancers to their stores to ensure a new year of prosperity.

In southern Mindanao, Muslims celebrate Hari Raya Puasa, the birth of the Prophet Muhammad, and Ramadan, the Muslim month of fasting.

INTERNET LINKS

http://news.xinhuanet.com/english2010/photo/2011-06/24/c_13948441.htm
This site contains lovely photos of the Taong Putik festival.

www.byahilo.com/2011/04/15/kadawayan-sa-davao-2011-schedule/#axzz1R7Kba7T5
This website includes interesting pictures of the Kadayawan festival in Davao.

www.philippinecountry.com/philippine_festivals/santacruzan.html
This is a comprehensive page on the Flores de Mayo festival with breathtaking pictures.

Rizal Park, also known as Luneta Park, is a historical urban park located at the northern terminus of Roxas Boulevard in the heart of the city of Manila, in honor of José Rizal.

FOOD

Vendors selling tropical fruits at a Carbon Market in Cebu city.

13

THE STAPLE FOOD OF THE Philippines is rice, the main agricultural crop. Fish harvested from the country's long shoreline complements rice in the Filipino's basic meal.

The traditional meal combines ingredients derived from the immediate surroundings, and cooking methods are simple. Fish and meat can be stewed with string beans, radishes, and soured tamarind or indigenous lemon.

Coconut and sugar are abundant and thus constitute a major part of the Philippine diet. Coconut milk is used to cook fish, meat, or vegetables, while its flesh can be candied or mixed in fruit salads. Filipinos have developed an incorrigible sweet tooth. A meal is never complete without a dessert—the sweeter the better.

In comparison with the spicy food of Southeast Asia, Philippine food is sometimes bland, but it is perfect for the sensitive palate. Filipinos do, however, like their food a little salty.

A MIXED TABLE

Philippine cuisine is as mixed as Filipino ancestry. The national diet includes many dishes of foreign origin, often adapted to suit the Filipino palate. Many indigenous foods have in turn been influenced by the cooking styles of the Malay immigrants, the Chinese traders, and the Western colonizers.

The Spanish component in the Philippine diet is strongest. From Spain, the Philippines inherited dishes such as *morcon* (MOR-kon),

Today Philippine cuisine continues to evolve as new techniques, styles of cooking, and ingredients find their way into the country. Traditional dishes, both simple and elaborate, indigenous and foreign-influenced, are seen, as are the more current popular international *viands* (VAHY-uh-nds) and fast-food fare.

121

beef stuffed with pork fat; *pochero* (put-CHAY-roh), beef, chicken, and pork chunks stewed with cabbage, green beans, and Spanish sausage; and that great culinary delight called *paella* (pah-AY-lah), a combination of rice, seafood, and meat.

From the Chinese came all sorts of noodles, or *pancit* (PAHN-sit). Filipinos have localized Chinese noodle dishes, creating hybrids such as *pancit palabok* (PAH-lah-book) and *pancit malabon* (MAH-lah-bon). Other Chinese foods popular in the Philippines are rice porridge, meat buns, spring rolls, and pastries filled with red beans or lotus seeds.

The Americans introduced refrigerators and ovens as well as salads, pies, hamburgers, and canned food. Italian spaghetti, sweetened for Filipino taste buds, is considered party fare.

Most indigenous concoctions come in the form of *kakanin* (KAH-kah-nin), a variety of rice cakes. Some dishes are distinctly national: *adobo* (ah-DO-boh), a dark stew of chicken and pork; *dinuguan* (DEE-noo-gwan), stew cooked in pig's blood; *bagoong* (BAH-goong), a shrimp paste with an off-putting smell; and *balut* (BAH-lut), boiled duck's egg with a half-formed chick. The latter two are formidable for those who have not acquired the taste, and eating them is considered the ultimate test of a foreigner's adjustment to Philippine life. Some more exotic dishes are *camaro* (KAR-ma-ro), which are field crickets cooked in soy sauce, salt, and vinegar as it is popular in Pampanga; *papaitan* (PAH-pay-ton), which is goat or beef innards stew flavored with bile that gives it a bitter taste; Soup No. 5 (also written as "Soup #5"), which is a soup made out of bull's testes; and *asocena* (AH-soh-ken-a) or dog meat, popular in the Cordillera Administrative Region.

RICE

The first thing Filipino children learn in the kitchen is how to cook rice. They wash the grain in a pot and fill the pot with water up to the second joint of the middle finger. Then they set the pot over low heat. They learn when to turn off the heat—not too early, not too late—and how long to leave the rice to steam before serving.

Rice served as a staple is usually boiled or fried; for special occasions, rice is cooked in different ways. Glutinous rice is baked to make a hundred kinds of *kakanin* (KAH-kah-nin). The most popular rice cake at Christmas is *bibingka* (bi-BING-kah), which is rice with coconut, egg, and milk baked in a clay oven.

Almost every province has its own *suman* (SOO-mahn), wrapped in coconut or banana leaf. The wrapper is a work of art that adds to the fragrance of the filling. The *pandan* (PAHN-dun) leaf of the pandanus plant, a screw pine, is often used when steaming rice and making desserts. The leaf gives food a special fragrance, flavor, and color.

Varieties of rice on sale at Baguio public market.

Rice mixed with cocoa is a child's favorite snack, usually eaten with something salty like dried fish. Ground rice is a necessary ingredient in other rice-based dishes such as steamed rice cakes, rice balls in sweet coconut milk, and rice cooked in sugar.

Palitaw (PAH-lee-tao) is a rice cake eaten with grated coconut and aniseeds. Rice gruel is generally fed to the sick; it may also be combined with chicken or tripe to make an enjoyable meal.

EATING RITUALS

For Filipinos, food not only feeds the body but the soul as well. Eating is a ritual that allows one to touch base with family and friends. There is hardly an occasion when food is not served. A casual neighborly visit can bring out a tray of spring rolls or a plate of noodles. Shopping, watching a basketball game on television, or even keeping vigil at a wake are all opportunities to share food.

Most Filipinos eat with a fork and a spoon. However, certain foods are best eaten using the fingers—fried rice and dried fish.

It is normal for Filipinos to share their food with others. If the person sitting next to you on the bus opens a bag of potato chips, he or she will offer you some. Houseguests are always served food and drinks, and if they come

A streetside
food stall.

unannounced in the middle of a meal, they will be asked to join in. It would probably be uncomfortable for the host if he or she had not cooked anything special that day, so the guests may considerately decline. But they will oblige if the host insists so as not to hurt his or her feelings.

WHERE TO EAT

Restaurants in Manila serve food from many cultures—Italian, French, Spanish, Indian, Thai, Vietnamese—to satisfy the healthy Filipino appetite. Although in the past eating out was a novel chance to experience foreign tastes, today indigenous fare has taken on its own glamour with the introduction of elegant restaurants serving indigenous food. Tourists are attracted to the exotic ambience of such places; some restaurants even encourage their customers to eat using their fingers! Wooden or wicker plates lined with banana leaves and coconut juice served in the coconut shell add to the novelty.

If it is regional fare one craves, then fancy restaurants are not the place to go, according to food critics. Instead it is the roadside stalls patronized by jeepney drivers and manual laborers that serve the most authentic regional fare.

Of course, patrons at roadside stalls do not enjoy the kind of service and atmosphere that cafés and restaurants offer. At roadside stalls, the customer chooses from an array of dishes behind a glass compartment, and the vendor piles the portions on a plate for the customer to take to a table and eat. Cart hawkers sell hot noodles and porridge at very low prices. Cola comes in bottles or may be poured into a plastic bag with a straw inserted.

In the market areas, competition is so stiff that vendors employ criers to cajole—maybe even force—customers to buy from their stalls. Sitting between two fierce criers can be quite an uncomfortable experience.

DESSERT ANYTIME

To satisfy their sweet tooth, Filipinos have concocted a variety of puddings, cakes, cookies, candies, flans, and other desserts. Here is a mouthwatering selection:

- bibingka—*glutinous rice cakes with a variety of toppings: fresh grated coconut, coconut cream, corn kernels, cottage cheese, white cheese, cheese strips, melted cheese*
- ginatan *(GHEE-na-tahn)*—*yam, sweet potato, and banana in coconut milk*
- halo-halo *(HA-lo-HA-lo)*—*beans, sago, banana, yam, and gelatin in crushed ice and milk*
- leche flan *(LET-che flahn)*—*baked egg custard*
- mais con hielo *(MAH-ees kon YEH-lo)*—*sweet corn kernels in crushed ice and milk*
- maruya *(MAH-ro-yah)*—*banana slices dipped in a batter of flour, egg, milk, and butter, then deep fried and rolled in sugar*
- pastillas de leche *(pas-TEE-liahs deh LET-cheh)*—*candied carabao milk*
- sorbetes *(SOR-veh-tehs)*—*local ice cream*
- suman *(SOO-mahn)*—*rice cake wrapped in coconut or banana leaf*
- ube *(OO-beh)*—*yam with milk*
- yema *(YEH-mah)*—*candy made from egg yolk and milk*

And in case there is a shortage of homemade desserts, different kinds of fruit preserves and jams from the supermarket are stocked in the kitchen cabinet.

NO TIME TO EAT

To Filipinos, eating is a serious matter, and time is taken to savor meals. But with the fast pace of urban life, quick meals are often the way to go. The roadside stalls are perhaps the cheapest and most convenient places to get one's daily meals. And of course, there is fast food—not only the original Western imports, but local versions as well.

Jollibee is a homegrown fast-food restaurant in the Philippines.

Fast-food outlets are found in every shopping mall, ready to feed hungry shoppers in a jiffy. Besides the established American chains such as McDonald's, there is the successful homegrown chain Jollibee. Fast-food stores even deliver, so people need not step out of their homes and offices for lunch or dinner. The delivery person brings ordered lunches into the office, and there are "back-ups" for other employees who have no time to wait in line at a cafeteria but have not placed orders with the restaurant in advance.

FIESTA FOOD

The fiesta is not just a social and religious event; it is also a culinary celebration. The fiesta table is a grand feast. It may feature such homey dishes as *dinuguan* or the sour soup *sinigang* (SI-nee-gahng), but with something extra to make it special for the occasion.

If there is one word that describes fiesta food, it is rich. Pork leg *estofado* (es-tuh-FAH-do) is simmered in burned sugar sauce and thickened with the nectar of ripe banana. An *embotido* (em-bo-TEE-do) is a steamed roll stuffed with egg, olives, relish, and ground meat. *Galantina* (gah-lahn-TEE-nah) is shredded or diced chicken flavored with broth, milk, and spices. *Lumpiang ubod* (LUMP-piang OOH-bod) is a spring roll filled with shrimp, pork, heart of palm, and only the softest coconut pith. The roll is sometimes topped with gravy seasoned with ground garlic. The *lapu-lapu* (LAH-po LAH-po) fish is steamed, then garnished with mayonnaise, relish, peas, corn, parsley, and shredded carrots.

The centerpiece of the fiesta spread is *lechón* (LET-son), a whole, four-month-old roasted pig with crunchy golden skin. Filipinos in Luzon eat *lechón* with a thick liver sauce; those in the Visayas prefer vinegar mixed with soy sauce and crushed chili.

No fiesta party is complete without a dessert. Leche flan, or egg custard, is made with duck's eggs for a creamy effect and immersed in burned sugar sauce. Gelatins in all colors, filled with raisins or tiny pieces of fresh fruit, are topped with whipped cream or milk. Soft and fluffy coconut strips are cooked with pandan leaves to create an aromatic preserve called *macapuno* (MAH-kah-POO-no).

FRUIT

Philippine fruit is mostly tropical. The most common are watermelon, papaya, avocado, soursop, jackfruit, mango, pineapple, guava, indigenous orange, and several varieties of banana. Some fruit is seasonal, such as rambutan and *siniguela* (si-nee-GWE-la), a green berry; some fruit is regional—for example, strawberries grow only in the cool highlands of the Mountain province, while Mindanao is the exclusive domain of the mangosteen and durian.

Fruit is eaten mostly as a dessert or snack, but it also has medicinal and superstitious value. For example, papaya is a cure for constipation, while banana is a good source of dietary fiber; guava can cause appendicitis and

A wide variety of tropical fruit is available in the Philippines.

siniguela can cause diarrhea. Expectant mothers crave green mango, but they stay away from *duhat* (DO-haht), a black cherry, believing that it will give the baby a dark complexion.

KITCHEN UTENSILS

The traditional Philippine kitchen is equipped with an earthen pot, a bamboo dipper, and a Chinese wok. It is believed that rice is best cooked in an earthen pot; the pores in the clay are said to preserve the flavor of the rice. Water is stored in a large clay jar. Older Filipinos swear that water from the jar is sweeter and fresher than water from the tap.

Ingredients used to make rice cakes are pounded in a heavy stone grinder. The *sandok* (SUN-dok), made of half a coconut shell tied to a stick, is the indigenous ladle. The *kawali* (kah-WALL-ih), or Chinese wok, is used for frying. A bigger version, the *kawa* (KAH-wah), is used at fiesta time in order to cook enough for the large party. Food is prepared on a bamboo table or on a *paminggalan* (PAH-ming-gah-lahn) where plates and glasses are left to dry.

Traditional kitchen equipment is not convenient for the fast pace of urban life. Modern technology has made the preparation of everyday meals a snap. The seconds-to-minutes microwave oven has replaced the gas stove, and the electric blender has replaced the cumbersome stone grinder.

OF FILIPINOS AND SPIRITS

When Magellan set out to fight that upstart of a chieftain, Lapu-Lapu, he and his men had just been to a feast where they drank a sweetish liquid that put them in high spirits. Strangely, before the day was over, Magellan and his men were defeated.

The drink that Magellan had was *tuba* (TOO-bah). It is still drunk today, a wine made from the sap of an unopened coconut bud. The tip of the bud is lopped off, and the sap is left to flow for a whole day. Tree bark is mixed with the sap, giving it a reddish hue.

Lambanog (lahm-buh-noog) is a powerful, clear distilled liquid that burns as it goes down the gullet. It is made from coconut fermented in a bottle with chewing gum and apples or raisins for a month. *Tuba* and *lambanog* are popular in coconut-producing provinces such as Laguna, Batangas, and Quezon.

Up north, the Ilocano ferment sugarcane sap in huge jars buried under their houses. The product is a wine called *basi* (bah-see). The Bontoc and Ifugao make rice wine called *tapuy* (TAH-pui).

Not to be outdone by the West, Filipinos have concocted their own beer, the internationally acknowledged San Miguel brand. There are also a few Philippine brands of rum, such as Manila Dark Rum and Tanduay Rum. The latter has won international renown and is one of the world's best-selling brands of rum. Tapuy is a traditional Philippine alcoholic drink made from fermented glutinous rice. It is a clear wine of luxurious alcoholic taste, moderate sweetness, and lingering finish. Its average alcohol content is 14 percent, or 28 proof, and does not contain any preservatives or sugar.

Trust a Filipino to find a place and time for a couple of drinks. In the spirit of camaraderie, a group of men share a bottle of liquor on a street corner. Each takes a shot, called a *tagay* (TAH-gai). Refusing a *tagay* embarrasses the person offering the drink, and this may lead to a brawl. Women in the countryside can gulp down a glassful of liquor without batting an eye; some can even outdrink their male counterparts.

INTERNET LINKS

http://visualrecipes.com/recipes/filipino/
This fantastic website has step-by-step picture guides on how to make various Filipino recipes.

www.asiarecipe.com/philippines.html
This site contains interesting Filipino recipes to try.

To increase the awareness of *tapuy*, the Philippine Rice Research Institute created a cookbook containing recipes and cocktails from famous Philippine chefs and bartenders, featuring *tapuy* as one of the ingredients.

PAELLA

This recipe serves 10 to 12 persons.

1 pound (500 g) chicken, cut into pieces

½ pound (250 g) pork, cut into pieces

Salt and pepper

Vegetable oil

1 pound (500 g) large shrimp, boiled

12 clams

2 garlic cloves, minced

2 tablespoons (30 ml) olive oil

1 medium-sized onion, sliced

3 cups (750 ml) roasted rice

3 cups (750 ml) chicken stock

½ cup (125 ml) tomato ketchup

½ cup (125 ml) water

1 piece Italian sausage, cooked and sliced

6 whole raw squid, cleaned

1 cup (250 ml) green peas

1 red pepper, sliced

Season chicken and pork with salt and pepper. Pan-fry in vegetable oil over medium heat until cooked, then set aside. Season shrimp with salt and pepper, then set aside. Boil clams until shell opens, then remove top and set aside. Fry garlic in olive oil until brown. Add onion, roasted rice, chicken stock, tomato ketchup, and water. Cover and bring to a boil. Reduce heat until the liquid evaporates and the rice is cooked. Garnish with remaining ingredients. Cover and simmer for 10 to 15 minutes.

LECHE FLAN

Ingredients

Caramel

1 cup (250 ml) sugar

1 cup (250 ml) water

Custard

12 egg yolks

1 can condensed milk

2 cups (500 ml) milk

1 tablespoon (15 ml) vanilla

Mix the water and sugar together in a saucepan on high heat. When the mixture has caramelized (it should turn a golden brown color), use it to line the ramekin (or loaf tin).

Pre-heat the oven to 375ºF (190ºC). Using a blender, blend all the ingredients for the custard. Pour the mixture into ramekin that has been lined with caramel. Cover with aluminium foil and place the ramekins into a larger baking tray that is half filled with water. Bake the flan for an hour or until the custard is firm. Once cooled, flip the ramekin over and pop the leche flan out and serve.

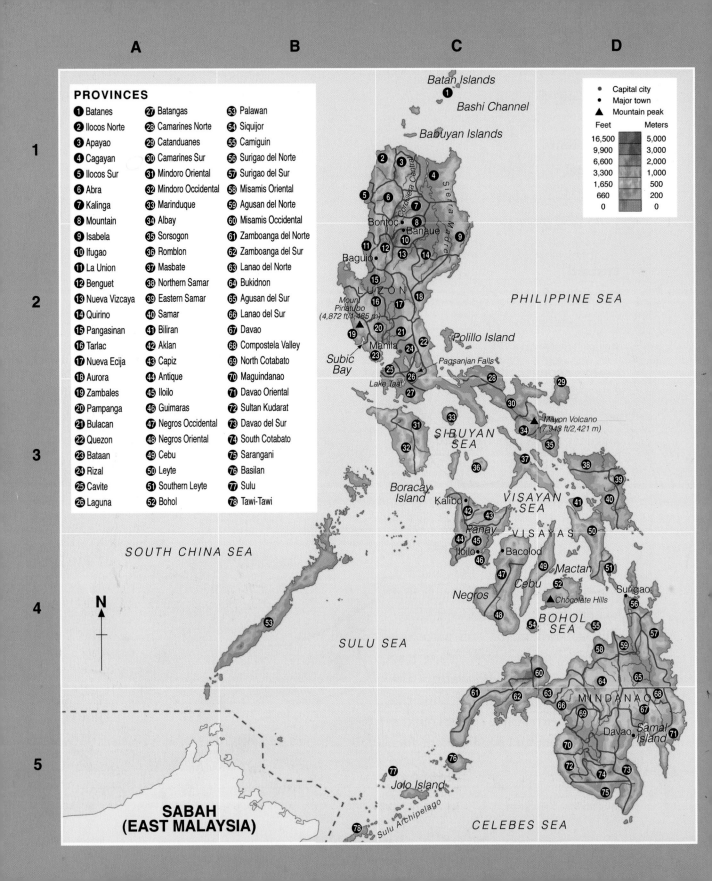

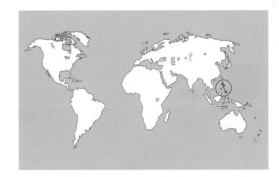

ECONOMIC PHILIPPINES

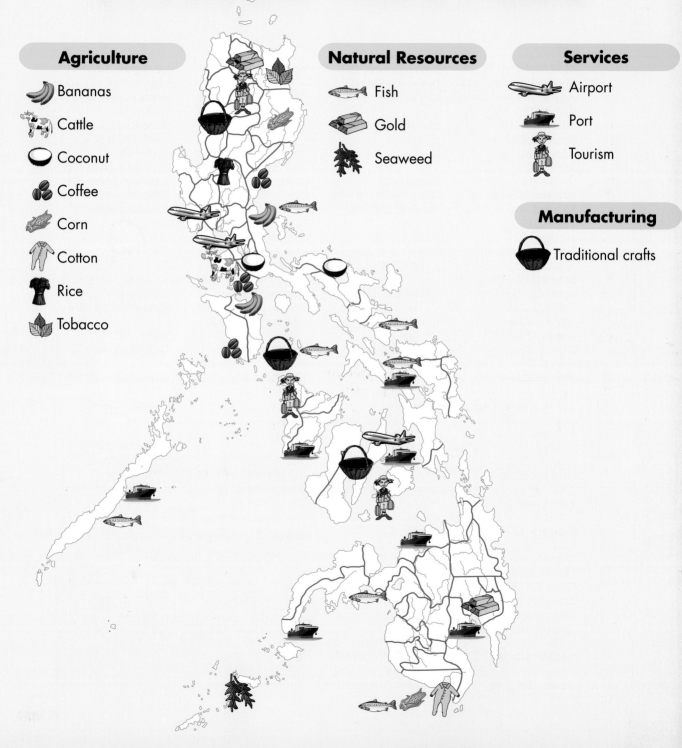

Agriculture

- Bananas
- Cattle
- Coconut
- Coffee
- Corn
- Cotton
- Rice
- Tobacco

Natural Resources

- Fish
- Gold
- Seaweed

Services

- Airport
- Port
- Tourism

Manufacturing

- Traditional crafts

ABOUT THE ECONOMY

OVERVIEW

The Philippine economy grew at its fastest pace in 2010, expanding 7.3 percent—this well surpassed the government's target of 5.0 percent to 6.0 percent and jumped from a growth of just 0.9 percent in 2009. The Philippines seeks to attract more foreign investment and enable the long underperforming economy to catch up with its fast-developing Asian neighbors, say analysts.

GROSS DOMESTIC PRODUCT

$351.4 billion (2010 estimate)

MAIN INDUSTRIES

Electronics assembly, garments, footwear, pharmaceuticals, chemicals, wood products, food processing, petroleum refining, fisheries and fishing, mining and natural resources, business process outsourcing

AGRICULTURAL PRODUCTS

Sugarcane, coconuts, rice, corn, bananas, cassavas, pineapples, mangoes, pork, eggs, beef, fish

CURRENCY

1 USD = 43.96 pesos (January 2012)
1 Philippine peso = 100 sentimos

IMPORTS

$59.9 billion (2010 estimate)

MAIN IMPORTS

Electronic products, mineral fuels, machinery and transport equipment, iron and steel, textile fabrics, grains, chemicals, plastics

EXPORTS

$50.72 billion (2010 estimate)

MAIN EXPORTS

Semiconductors and electronic products, transport equipment, garments, copper products, petroleum products, coconut oil, fruits

LABOR FORCE

38.9 million (2010 estimate)

UNEMPLOYMENT

7.3 percent (2010 estimate)

INFLATION

3.8 percent (2010 estimate)

TRADING PARTNERS

The United States, Japan, the Netherlands, China, Germany, Singapore, South Korea, Taiwan, Thailand

REGIONAL/INTERNATIONAL COOPERATION

The Philippines is a member of the World Trade Organization, Asia Pacific Economic Conference, and Association of Southeast Asian Nations.

CULTURAL PHILIPPINES

ANCESTRAL HOUSES

Vigan is home to 193 ancestral houses and historic buildings built in the late 1800s and early 1900s. The brick-and-plaster houses, with their red tiled roofs, grand doorways and staircases, broad floorboards, and sliding windows, display the ingenuity of indigenous craftsmen, who created a style suited to the demands of an earthquake-prone location.

KABAYAN MUMMIES

The mummified bodies of Ibaloi royalty were found in caves around Kabayan in the early 1990s. It is believed the mummies were made between A.D. 1200 and 1500. Animal-shaped coffins and artifacts such as pottery and clothing have also been discovered in the caves. It is likely that the Spanish arrival put a stop to the pratice of mummification.

INTRAMUROS

Manila's walled city is where Legaspi erected a fortress in 1571. Within lies Fort Santiago, housing the cell of José Rizal before his execution by the Spanish, and a marble cross marking the grave of 600 Filipinos and Americans killed by the Japanese in World War II. Also here is Manila's oldest fort and its Byzantine circular stone maze.

MALACAÑANG PALACE

The Palace has stood on the northern bank of the Pasig River as a symbol of power for three centuries. Once the official residence of the Spanish governor-general and later of the American civil governor, the Palace became the official residence of the Philippine president in 1935.

MORIONES FESTIVAL

This festival takes place in Marinduque during Holy Week. Participants wear painted papier-mâché masks and dress up as biblical figures. They reenact the story of a Roman centurion who converted to Christianity and was beheaded. The story goes that when he pierced the side of Jesus Christ, the blood touched and healed his blind eye.

TABON CAVES

This system of 29 caves in Quezon is known as the cradle of Philippine civilization. The caves hid the secrets of the earliest Filipinos until 1962, when a team discovered the 22,000-year-old fossils of the Tabon Man.

WINDSURFERS' PARADISE

Boracay is the country's best-known windsurfing destination. With a large reef-rimmed lagoon, the island boasts windspeeds in the range of 10–30 miles per hour (18.5–55.6 km per hour) from December to April. The annual Boracay International Funboard Cup brings together sailors from around the world for six days of races and parties.

RICE TERRACES

The spectacular rice terraces around Banaue were carved out of the hillside by Ifugao cultivators 2,000 to 3,000 years ago. The terraces, some reaching 4,920 feet (1,500m), stretch like steps to the sky.

AYALA MUSEUM

This museum in Makati City promotes awareness and interest in Philippine culture and history through exhibits of historical artifacts and contemporary art and educational programs and publications.

BAMBOO ORGAN FESTIVAL

Every February, Las Piñas holds a week-long music festival revolving around an old 1,031-pipe bamboo organ 13 feet (4 m) in height and width. The organ was first built in the early 1800s and rebuilt after the 1896 revolution. In the 1970s, it was sent to Germany for restoration, then returned to Las Piñas. So began the annual festival.

NAYONG PILIPINO

Nayong Pilipino in Pasay City is the Philippines in miniature. The theme park highlights the country's regions and cultures. Museums exhibit the furniture, religious symbols, arts, and other belongings of the different ethnic groups. Gardens, an aquarium, and an aviary feature indigenous fish, bird, and plant life.

ATI-ATIHAN FESTIVAL

Held every January in Kalibo, the Ati-Atihan reminds the visitor of Mardi Gras. Celebrants dressed in bright costumes, faces painted with black soot, dance in lively processions and parades.

CHOCOLATE HILLS

More than 1,000 mysterious cone-shaped hills dot the land for miles in Bohol. The slopes of the hills are green in the rainy season, but turn a chocolate brown in summer when the grass dries.

ABOUT THE CULTURE

OFFICIAL NAME
Republic of the Philippines

FLAG
The national flag of the Philippines consists of a blue band on top, a red band at the bottom, and a white triangle based on the hoist edge. The center of the triangle features a yellow sun with eight rays representing the eight provinces that fought for independence from Spain. At each corner of the triangle is a yellow star representing one of the three main island groups.

NATIONAL ANTHEM
Lupang Hinirang (LOO-pahng hee-NEE-rahng)—"Ordained Land"

CAPITAL
Manila

MAJOR CITIES
Manila, Quezon, Davao, Cebu, and Baguio

MAIN ISLAND GROUPS
Luzon, Mindanao, and the Visayas

LITERACY RATE
93 percent (2011 estimate)

POPULATION
101.8 million (July 2011 estimate)
Luzon, the largest island group, is home to more than half the total population. Metro Manila has a population of some 20 million people, including the suburbs.

ETHNIC GROUPS (A SELECTION)
Apayao, Bagobo, Bontoc, Boholano, Cebuano, Ifugao, Ilocano, Kalinga, Mandaya, Manobo, Negrito (Aeta), Subanon, Tagalog, and T'boli

LANGUAGES
National: Filipino (based on Tagalog); Official: English; Bicolano, Cebuano, Hiligaynon, Ilocano, Kapam-pangan, Maguindanao, Tagalog, and Waray are the main regional languages or dialects.

RELIGIOUS GROUPS
Roman Catholics: 80.9 percent; Protestants: 7.3 percent; Muslims: 5 percent; Buddhists, Taoists, animists, and others make up the remaining 6.8 percent of the population.

HOLIDAYS
New Year's Day (January 1), Holy Week (March/April), Day of Valor (April 9), Labor Day (May 1), Independence Day (June 12), Manila Day (June 24), National Heroes' Day (Every last Monday of August), Bonifacio Day (November 30), Christmas Day (December 25), and Rizal Day (December 30)

TIME LINE

IN PHILIPPINES	IN THE WORLD
	1206–1368 Genghis Khan unifies the Mongols and starts conquest of the world. At its height, the Mongol Empire under Kublai Khan stretches from China to Persia and parts of Europe and Russia.
A.D. 1521 Portuguese explorer Ferdinand Magellan reaches Cebu Island.	
1565 Miguel Lopez de Legazpi establishes a Spanish colony on Cebu Island.	
1571 Manila is founded by Legazpi.	
1762 The British occupy Manila.	**1776** U.S. Declaration of Independence
	1789–99 The French Revolution
1872 Cavite conspiracy; José Rizal leads Propaganda Movement.	
1896 Rizal is executed.	
1898 Declaration of Independence; Spain cedes the Philippines to the United States for $20 million.	
1899 Aguinaldo proclaims the first Philippine Republic.	
1935 Start of the 10-year Commonwealth era	**1914** World War I begins.
1942 Manila falls to the Japanese.	**1939** World War II begins.
1944 U.S. forces regain Leyte; the Philippine Commonwealth is reestablished.	**1945** The United States drops atomic bombs on Hiroshima and Nagasaki. World War II ends.
1946 The United States grants the Philippines political independence.	
1965 Ferdinand Marcos is elected president; he is reelected four years later.	

IN PHILIPPINES	IN THE WORLD
1972 Marcos declares martial law.	
1985 Marcos calls for snap presidential elections; Corazon Aquino assumes the presidency.	
1992 Fidel Ramos is elected president; the last U.S. naval vessel leaves Subic.	
	1997 Hong Kong is returned to China.
1998 Joseph Estrada is elected president.	
2000 Gloria Arroyo is elected president.	
2001 Protest sparked by the arrest of Joseph Estrada. General elections are held.	**2001** Terrorists crash planes into New York, Washington D.C., and Pennsylvania.
2003 Oakwood mutiny—a group of 321 armed soldiers takes over the Oakwood Premier Ayala Center in Makati City to show the alleged corruption of the Gloria Macapagal-Arroyo administration.	**2003** War in Iraq begins.
2004 General elections are held; Gloria Macapagal-Arroyo is elected to a six-year term.	**2004** Eleven Asia countries are hit by giant tsunami, killing at least 225,000 people.
	2005 Hurricane Katrina devastates the Gulf Coast of the United States.
2006 A state of emergency is declared in February in response to coup rumors.	
2007 General elections are held.	
	2008 Earthquake in Sichuan, China, kills 67,000 people.
	2009 Outbreak of flu virus H1N1 around the world
2010 General elections are held; Benigno Aquino III wins. A hostage crisis in Manila results in eight Hong Kong tourists being killed. Typhoon Megi causes widespread damage in Luzon.	**2011** Twin earthquake and tsunami disasters strike northeast Japan, leaving more than 14,000 dead and thousands more missing.

GLOSSARY

amor propio (ah-MOR PRO-pio)
Self-esteem, similar to the concept of "face".

asuang (AS-wahng)
A creature of the underworld.

babaylan (BA-BY-lun)
A faith healer or shaman.

barangay (ba-RUNG-gai)
Originally a pre-Spanish Filipino community, now still the basic unit of the Philippine society and government.

barong (BA-rong)
Traditional wear for Filipino men.

barrio
A village.

cenaculo (si-NAH-KU-loh)
The Philippine version of the passion play performed during Holy Week.

compadrazgo (COM-pud-DRAS-co)
Non-blood kinship ties usually established for baptisms, weddings, or any kind of sponsorship.

delicadeza (DE-lee-ka-DE-za)
Social propriety.

Filipina
A female resident of the Philippines.

galleon
A Spanish ship that sailed between Manila and Acapulco, laden with goods for Spain.

hiya (HEE-ya)
Shame.

Indios
A derogatory term used by the Spanish colonial masters to refer to the indigenous Filipinos.

karaoke
A leisure activity where people sing using a microphone, guided by music and lyrics; also the club in which people do this.

kristo (KRIS-to)
The ringmaster at a cockfight.

Maria Clara
Dress worn by Filipinas, named after the main female character in José Rizal's *Noli Me Tangere*.

mestizos
People of mixed ancestry.

pakikisama (pa-KI-ki-SUM-ma)
The art of maintaining smooth interpersonal relationships.

pamanhikan (PA-man-HEE-khan)
A formal proposal for a woman's hand in marriage.

Pinoy (PEE-noi)
The Filipinos' nickname for themselves.

singkil (SING-kil)
The traditional Philippine bamboo dance.

viands (VAHY-uh-nds)
Articles of food.

FOR FURTHER INFORMATION

BOOKS

Bloom, Greg, Grosberg, Michael, Jealous, Virginia and Kelly, Piers. *Lonely Planet Philippines* (Country Travel Guide). California: Lonely Planet, 2009.

Fancy, Robin Lyn (Author), Welch, Vala Jeanne (Author), Gasmen, Imelda Fines (Editor), Lynn, Ronny (Illustrator) *My Filipino Word Book*, Honolulu, Hawaii: Bess Press, 2007.

Gasmen, Imelda Fines. *Tuttle Tagalog for Kids Flash Cards Kit* (Tuttle Flash Cards), Claredon, Vermont: Tuttle Publishing, 2008.

Gilmore, Dorina K. Lazo, and Valiant, Kristi. *Cora Cooks Pancit*. Walnut Creek, California: Shen's Books 2009.

Miller, John Maurice. *Philippines Folklore Stories*. Florida: General Books, 2010.

Olizon-Chikiamco, Norma (Author), Ramsel N. Salvatus III, Mark (Illustrator). *Pan de Sal Saves the Day: A Filipino Children's Story*. Claredon, Vermont: Tuttle Publishing, 2009.

Romulo, Liana and Dandan-Albano, Corazon. *Filipino Friends*. Claredon, Vermont: Tuttle Publishing,   2006.

Romulo, Liana and Laurel, Jamie. *My First Book of Tagalog Words: Filipino Rhymes and Verses*. Claredon, Vermont: Tuttle Publishing, 2007.

Yuson, Alfred A., Tapan, and George. *Philippines: Islands of Enchantment*. Claredon, Vermont: Tuttle Publishing, 2010.

WEBSITES

Asian Development Bank Philippines. www.adb.org/philippines/main.asp

Theodora.com—Philippines. www.theodora.com/wfbcurrent/philippines/

Library of Congress Country Study: Philippines. http://memory.loc.gov/frd/cs/phtoc.html

Lonely Planet World Guide: Destination Philippines. www.lonelyplanet.com/philippines

National Geographic News "Still Green in Luzon." http://news.nationalgeographic.com/news/2000/12/1214_subicbay.html

National Statistical Coordination Board. www.nscb.gov.ph

Philippine culture and information. http://pinas.dlsu.edu.ph/culture/culture.html

Philippine Department of Tourism. www.tourism.gov.ph

MUSIC

Paraiso. Florante Aguilar & Lori Abucayan, New Art Media, August 2007

Popular Guitar Music of the Philippines. Ric Ickard, Naxos, July 2006

Tipanan—A Celebration of the Philippine Guitar. Florante Aguilar, New Art Media, August 2006

DVDs

Globe Trekker—The Philippines. Pilot Productions, January 2010

Travelview International Philippines. TravelVideoStore.com, November 2009

BIBLIOGRAPHY

BOOKS

Bloom, Greg, Grosberg, Michael, Jealous, Virginia and Kelly, Piers. *Lonely Planet Philippines (Country Travel Guide)*. California: Lonely Planet, 2009.

Hicks, Nigel. *Philippines Travel Pack*, 5th (Globetrotter Travel Packs). Middlesex, England: Globetrotter, 2010.

Roces, Alfredo and Roces, Grace. *Culture Shock! Philippines: A Survival Guide to Customs and Etiquette*. Tarrytown, New York: Marshall Cavendish Reference, 2009.

Worchester, Dean C. *The Philippines, Past and Present*, Volume 1 & 2. Qontro Classic Books, 2010.

Yuson, Alfred A., and Tapan, George. *Philippines: Islands of Enchantment*. Claredon, Vermont: Tuttle Publishing, 2010.

WEBSITES

Country Studies—U.S.: Philippines. http://countrystudies.us/philippines/45.htm

Culture of the Philippines. www.everyculture.com/No-Sa/The-Philippines.html

eTravelPhilipinas. www.etravelpilipinas.com/about_philippines/philippine_culture.htm

Filipino Recipes. www.filipinofoodrecipes.net/

http://tagaloglang.com/Filipino-Culture/Religion/religion-in-the-philippines.html

Infoplease—Philippines. www.infoplease.com/ipa/A0107887.html

Lonely Planet—Philippines. www.lonelyplanet.com/philippines

Official Gazette of the Republic of the Philippines. www.gov.ph/

Philippines Cultural and Folk Dances. http://philippinesculturalfolkdances.blogspot.com/

Philippines Culture. www.marimari.com.my/content/philippines/best_of/culture.html

Philippines Culture, Customs and Traditions. www.cebu-philippines.net/philippine-culture.html

Philippines Dance. www.camperspoint.com/spip.php?article229

Philippines Folk Dances. www.philippine-travel-guide.com/philippine-folk-dances.html

Philippines Food. www.asiarecipe.com/philippines.html

Religion in Philippines. www.asiarooms.com/en/travel-guide/philippines/culture-of-philippines/religion-in-philippines.html

Religion in the Philippines. http://tagaloglang.com/Filipino-Culture/Religion/religion-in-the-philippines.html

The Official Website of the Republic of the Philippines. http://dfa.gov.ph/main/

The Philippines. www.philippines.hvu.nl/

U.S. Department of State—Philippines. www.state.gov/r/pa/ei/bgn/2794.htm

WOW Philippines. www.tourism.gov.ph

INDEX

INDEX